Signed

Henry Burstow

1912

Yours Faithfully

Henry Burstow

Reminiscences of HORSHAM,

being

Recollections of

Henry Burstow

The celebrated Bellringer & Songsinger.

With some account of the Old Bell Foundry at Horsham, Of the Horsham Parish Church Bells. and Of famous Peals rung by Horsham Ringers.

Together with a list of the 400 and odd Songs he sings from memory.

Published by the Free Christian Church Book Soc.ty Worthing Road, Horsham.
Sep.r 1911.

LIST OF ILLUSTRATIONS.

———

A

HORSHAM:

PRINTED BY S. PRICE & CO., 48, WEST STREET.

1911.

INTRODUCTION.

IN deciding to compose and publish this little book the writer had but one object in view, viz.: that of rendering help to old HENRY BURSTOW, Horsham's famous Bellringer and Song Singer, who, in the declining years of his long life, with neither son nor daughter, and but few friends able to help him, was found to be in indigent circumstances. To most Horsham people HENRY BURSTOW is well known, but there will probably be many readers of these pages to whom he is a stranger, and to whom, therefore, an introduction will not be superfluous; whilst to all readers, and especially subscribers, the writer feels he ought to give an explanation of, if not an apology for, his solicitation of their support.

HENRY BURSTOW was born and brought up in a humble sphere, and started in a path that rewarded constant hard work with but poor pay. He pursued this path, working early and late, maintaining himself, and later his wife, and getting in return for his labour but a mere subsistence wage sufficient only for food, clothes, and house rent week by week. Concurrently he indulged his hobbies: Church bellringing, which, whilst touching the sentiments of thousands who love the fabric, and perhaps the doctrines, of the Church, and making him famous near and far, added but little to his income; and song singing, which, whilst enlivening many a jolly evening, preserving many good folk songs, and adding to his fame, was still less useful to him as a source of profit. He also found time to indulge, in a lesser degree, in bird fancying and water-colour painting. Two specimens of the latter, "Collyer's Free School" and "The Sussex County Gaol," will be found in this book.

Perhaps it was this humble occupation and the enjoyment of these hobbies, together with his excellent health and spirits, that provided a suitable environment for the cultivation and preservation of those qualities that have commanded the respect of his fellow townsmen, and continue to radiate in so charming a manner from his old age; his cheerful temperament, generous disposition, delight in thinking and doing good without hope of reward, firmness in shunning evil without the pressure of fear of punishment, enjoyment of life to the last, fearlessness of death whenever it may come. A truth and peace-loving Humanitarian, an honest and bold Freethinker, he has maintained through life a disposition that never earned him an enemy; a cherry optimism that has warmed the hearts of all who have come into contact with him, and a character that would have adorned many a highly-placed dignitary did he possess it.

Those who might say he ought to have provided for his old age may refer to page 23, where he gives the amount of wages he received for his labour, and may reflect that had he died at the end of the so-called span of life—threescore years and ten—he would have been dependent neither upon charity nor the sale of this book; and further, that by any just and scientific system of the distribution of wealth instead of the "get-what-you-can" principle that has obtained through his life, and has dealt out but too frequently large fortunes to sharp rogues and penury to honest toilers; by any such system he would have received ample provision for his old age and been free from the anxiety that always haunts the sensitive nature when in the bond or region of poverty.

It seemed something of a reproach that one with such a character, one so widely known by means of his fame as a bellringer and song singer, should suffer distress through being deprived by ruthless age of the ability to earn his living, which, with the willingness he still possesses, he exercised for as many years of his long life as possible; and so, knowing what an excellent memory he possessed, and also that he had lived all his life in his native town, the writer took down his recollections in the hope that if and when published they might be sufficiently interesting to sell and produce a profit for his benefit.

Mr. BURSTOW's statements have been corroborated where access to documentary evidence respecting them has been obtained. A search of records has not only verified and amplified many of his statements, but has also furnished much other interesting information, including particulars of the Sussex Assizes, of public executions by hanging and burning, of smuggling, of barrack life, of electioneering, and of the old Court Leet system of local government, &c., all concerning the town of Horsham. This matter, which is quite outside Mr. Burstow's knowledge, it was intended to publish, together with his recollections; but his advancing age and declining strength, and the delay, to say nothing of the greater expense involved in putting it into consecutive and readable form, make it advisable that his recollections be published alone, and as soon as possible; hence the present little volume.

It may be thought by some readers that too much mention is made of the drunkenness that disfigured many of the events and episodes of which accounts are given. The question whether inclusion or omission of such unpleasant facts is the better is, perhaps, a debatable one, but as this little book is something of an attempt to give a picture of Horsham of from forty to eighty years ago, the writer, with a view to correctness and completeness has thought it advisable to include the alcoholic colour. The disappointment, too, caused by his inability to find documentary evidence of many interesting tales about Horsham has been a further inducement to put the facts on record, rather than leave them to the doubtful care of tradition, For instance, it is said that in former times gambling for large stakes was prevalent at Horsham, and that the peculiar intricacies of some of the properties in the Town resulted from winnings and losings at the gaming table. Sometimes the ownership of a room or two rooms of a house would, by card playing, be changed, and the room or rooms be transferred to the owner of the adjoining house. Records of these transactions would be much more satisfactory than mere tradition, however well founded, but no such records as far as the writer is aware are available. If the inclusion of the un-pleasant facts alluded to give offence to those who like the truth shaped to their fancy, it will give satisfaction to those who would rather look back upon things as they actually were, than as they would like them to have been. Youthful readers may think the colour is laid on too thickly; such, however, is not the case, it could truthfully have been deepened. Those who knew Horsham thirty or forty years ago can see a great improvement in the habits of the people, whilst those whose recollections go further are well aware that the

Town's evil reputation in this matter was only too well-earned.

It seems usual to include in the preface to a book either an apology for its production or a positive statement that no apology is needed. Having regard to the object in issuing this book, and the great interest that items of local information have for all whose sentiments are attached to the old Town of Horsham, an apology is perhaps due; but not from the writer. It is due rather from those who, with greater leisure and talents, and higher training, are better equipped for making such a publication more profitable, more readable, and more valuable to the local topographer. Conscious as the writer is of its many errors, not of statement but of workmanship, which deprive it of all value as a literary production, he feels it had better appear with its blemishes than not at all. Of those able and disposed to criticise he must ask mercy; to those who like doing a good turn no more need be said.

The writer begs to express his thanks to many people for their kind assistance, especially to Mr. Wm. H. Blaber, of Hove, who kindly gave him access to valuable papers; Mr. R. Garraway-Rice, J.P., F.S.A., of Pulborough, who kindly allowed him to quote fully from his publication "Some account of Richard Eldridge, of Horsham," and "Notes upon the Bells of St. Mary's Church"; to his (the writer's) uncle, Mr. Edward Aldridge, of London, late of Horsham; to Mr. John Robinson, Mr. Geo. Lovekin, Mr. John Peters, and Mrs. Richard Bourn, all of Horsham; Mr. Charles West and Mrs. W. Roberts, both of Brighton, late of Horsham; Miss Lucy Broadwood, Hon. Sec. of the Folk Song Society; Mr. Tom Charman, and many other people either for information or corroboration; to Mr. T. Gurney Stedman for encouragement and help ; and to the Worthing Road Book Society, which, as a result of his reading portions of the Reminiscences to some of its members, kindly undertook their publication.

The matter then is given to the printer with diffidence, yet with hope that it may in some degree achieve the object in writing it. If, in addition, it should be thought sufficiently interesting to be given a humble place in local libraries, the writer will feel amply repaid for many hours given to a somewhat trying but congenial task.

18, LONDON ROAD,
        HORSHAM,
                September, 1911.

MAP OF HORSHAM, 1831 (the thick dotted lines shew the boundary of the old Borough; these, with the thin dotted lines, shew the boundary of the Borough and Town).

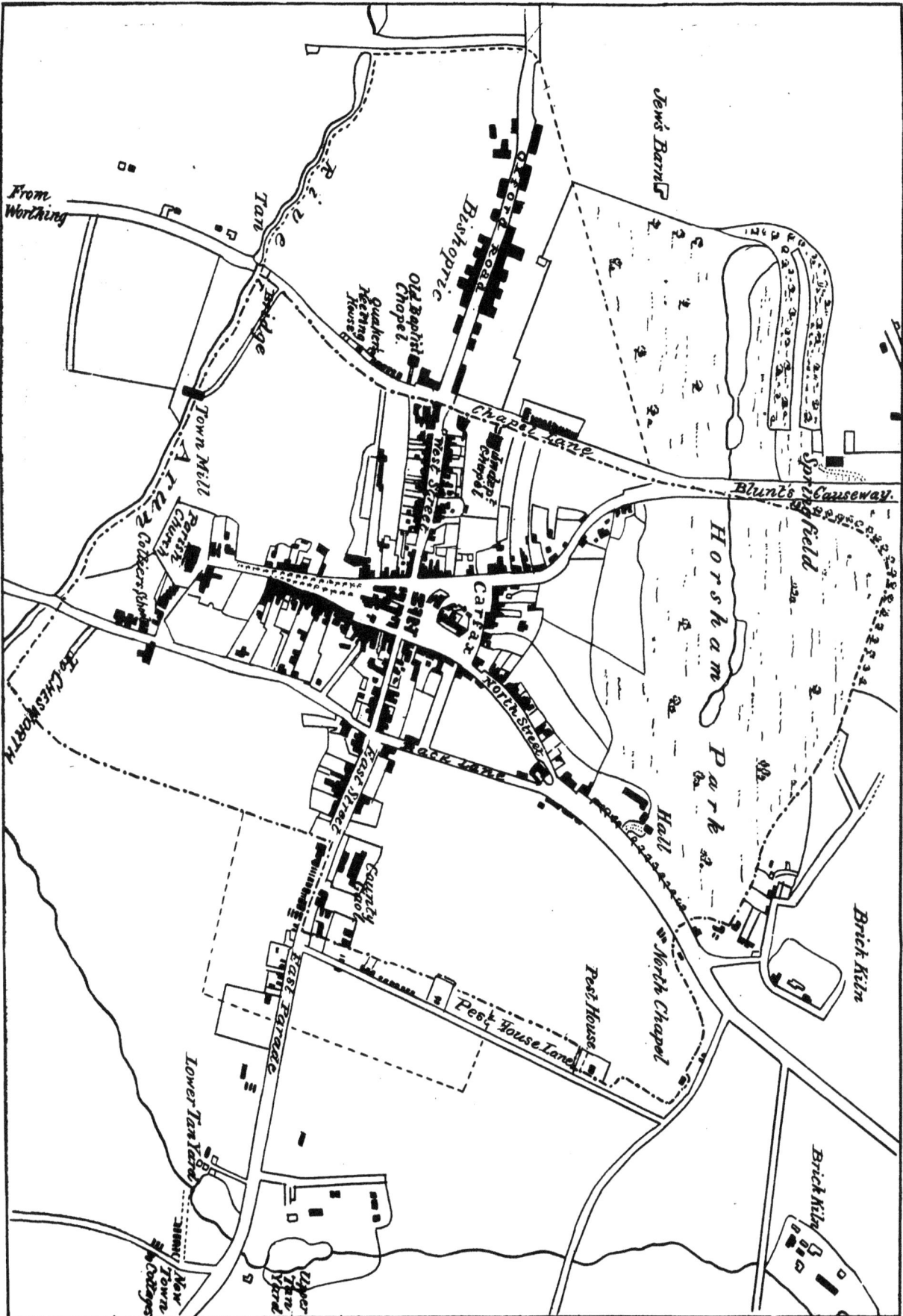

From Worthing

Jews Barn

Bishopric

Oxford Road

Old Baptist Chapel.

Quakers Meeting House

Tan

Bridge

Chapel Lane

Independt Chapel

Blunt's Causeway.

Springfield

Town Mill

Parish Church

North Street

New Street

Horsham Park &c.

N Colbertstone

To Chesworth

Carfax

North Street

Back Lane

East Street

Hall

Horsham Park &c.

County Gaol

North Chapel

Brick Kiln

East Parade

Pest House Lane

Pest House

Lower Tan Yard

New Town Cottages

Upper Tan Yard

Brick Kiln

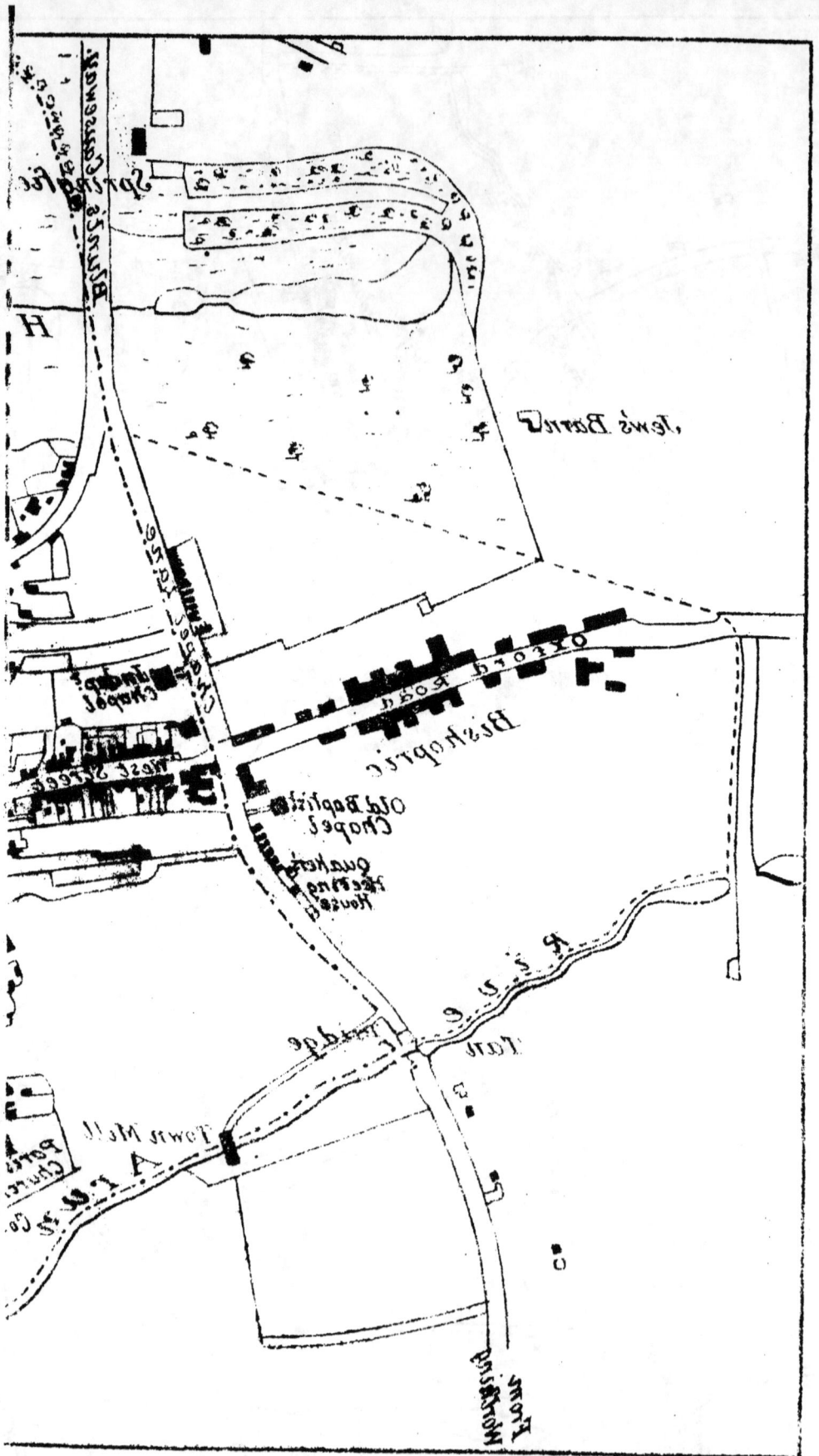

MAP OF HORSHAM, 1851: the thick dotted lines shew the boundary

REMINISCENCES OF HORSHAM.

RECOLLECTIONS OF HENRY BURSTOW.

I WAS born on Monday, the 11th Dec., 1826, in the house now known as No. 34, Bishopric, next door eastwards of the "Jolly Ploughboy" beershop. I was the next youngest of a family of nine children and lived there 42 years. My father, born on Wednesday, the 11th April, 1781, was a clay tobacco-pipe maker and moved into this house, which was his "factory," dwelling house and shop, in 1818 : he with my mother and some of the family were constantly employed making pipes, with which he at regular periods would travel in a pony cart round the neighbourhood to sell. My grandfather, also a pipemaker by trade, was born on the 13th Jan., 1721, and lived in a house that is now No. 50, East Street. When quite a young man he joined the Army and fought at the battle of Fontenoy in 1745. His father, my great-grandfather, was also a native of Horsham. He lived somewhere in North Street, and was a saddler and harness maker by trade. I never knew the date of his birth, but it must have been over 200 years ago, back in misty traditional times wherein his father is credited with having been a wealthy and popular burgess of the Town, owning considerable property in East Street. I regret, for the sake of those people whose tastes are offended by any literature not written by or about persons of proved blue-blooded descent, that I cannot either by record or tradition trace my genealogy back farther. Yet thus unable to assert that the Burstows came over with William the Conqueror or had a left-handed origin at the Court of Henry VIII. or Charles

B

II., we have been descending like the Plantagenet-Smythes for untold generations. In any case I hope I have made good my claim to the nativity of dear old Horsham, and that my position in the estimation of my fellow-townsmen is higher than it could be made by pedigree alone; for after all he is a poor creature that relies for his character upon, and attempts to borrow lustre from the reputations of his progenitors.

There has always been a doubt as to the origin of the name of Horsham, but no such doubt attaches to the origin of the popular name of that part of the Town in which I was born, "The Rookery." One tradition credits it to the fact that at one time rooks used to build their nests in an avenue of tall trees there; but candour compels me to refute this pleasing error and replace it with an explanation less creditable. In my young days the Bishopric was the roughest quarter in the Town and many respectable residents disliked going there after dark for fear of being molested. The name "Rookery" sprang from one of the numerous fights and squabbles that used to disgrace the neighbourhood. One day a woman from another part of the Town came down to settle an outstanding score with a Bishopric woman: during the fight several other Bishopric women came to the help of their sister and gave the intruder a lively time of it. "Yah!!" she halloed at them as she was driven off, "you are like a lot of d——d old rooks; if you upset one you upset the lot." In my father's young days The Bishopric was also known as lower West Street and had an open ditch or sewer running down the south side of it with here and there a rough stone bridge over to give access to the old cottages lying back on that side of the road. As long ago as I can remember it was also called the Oxford Road. Springfield Road was called Chapel Lane, Worthing

Road was also known as The Barracks way, Middle Street was also called Butcher's Row, the Carfax was also known as Gaol Green, Park Street was called Back Lane, and New Street was called Pesthouse Lane, after the isolation house there for infectious diseases, and the entrance to the little *cul de sac* in the Normandy was known as Hell Corner.

Very soon after I was born I began to develop a faculty with which I may say, without boasting, I was endowed in an extraordinary degree. I inherited a tenacious memory, to which from babyhood upwards I committed particulars of numerous events and incidents, tales, and songs: once my observations, mental or visual, were made and committed to memory, nothing has been able to dispossess me of them. The mental pictures I drew of the tales and songs taught me by my father, even before I was as high as the table, and the words of all the songs he taught me (those starred in the list at the end of this book), as well as the whole four hundred and odd songs there named, all these I have in my mind and on my tongue to-day. This faculty has been especially useful to me in my career as a change bell-ringer, an occupation that imposes a severe tax upon the memory, and I am much in hopes that its usefulness in recording the following particulars of Horsham in my younger days may be appreciated by my fellow townsmen.

The first thing that I can remember was my lying in my cradle, which was being rocked by my elder sister's foot, immaturely contemplating the ceiling of our little living room. I can remember, too, the time when, too young yet to walk, I was carried in my sister's arms when she went up town shopping. Perambulators or baby carriages were quite unknown, so I am unable to give an infant's appreciation of riding in state; but I can distinctly remember my infant experiences in learning to walk. I can now almost feel round my waist the sash to which the cord used for leading me was fastened. Sometimes this cord was fixed to a staple in a beam across the ceiling, giving me tethered experiences in pedestrianism I have never forgotten.

Our little cottage contained but one common living room, about 11ft. × 11ft. and about 6ft. 6in. high, with the front door opening to the street; the kitchen and scullery on the ground floor; and three small bedrooms upstairs; a small back yard, not large enough to grow anything, and the usual offices, completed the premises, the rent of which was 2s. 6d. per week. In the living room was the down fireplace, upon which my mother would burn nothing but wood, sharing a local prejudice, which was very strong, against coal; "nasty black stuff," she used to say, "you can't touch it for soot!" Against the west wall stood our chief piece of furniture, a plain square table, with drop leaves. This, at all meal times, was brought out to the middle of the room for us all to sit round and eat from. In one corner stood a small round table, over which was a corner cupboard; six chairs placed here and there; a few cheap prints, chief of which was a biblical set illustrating episodes in the life of Joseph, decorated the walls, bare of paper; a few other gimcracks, and the bench upon which my mother used to help make the pipes! these completed the items of furniture in our best room, and became the first objects of my baby stocktaking.

The rent of the cottage, small as the latter was, and still is, may seem low to the present generation, but other necessaries were very dear as compared with to-day's prices. Most tradespeople and cottagers made all the bread the family ate, and they, especially the cottagers, frequently found it a hard job to make enough. The price of flour varied very considerably. It used to be reckoned that it should always be the same number of pence per gallon as wheat was pounds per load. Horsham maintained a splendid reputation as a wheat growing centre, but prices were very unsteady, fluctuating sometimes violently between £12 and £45 per load in the Horsham Market. Farmers would refuse good prices in the hopes of shortly getting better, whilst labourers would frequently find the whole of their wages did not suffice to provide themselves, wives, and families with bread. I have known of farmers refusing £40 per load, expecting the price to rise by the following week; and I have heard of labourers' wives who, expecting to increase their family, have been reduced to the necessity of stealing turnips from the fields, at night time, to sustain life. Moist sugar was 6d. to 8d. per lb.; other groceries and provisions were equally high in price. Butchers meat we rarely tasted, whilst the prohibitive price of tea, 6s. and 8s. to 10s. per lb., made us feel very grateful when we could get the tea leaves second-hand, as my mother sometimes did from Mrs. Marriott, a kind old lady who then lived at Tanfield. The brilliant lighting powers of paraffin and gas were not in use in my infant days. In the larger houses, lamps burning spern oil at 5s. or 6s. per gallon, or whale oil at 3s. 6d. per gallon, spluttered and emitted bad smells; even cotton tallow candles were luxuries we could not afford. Common rushes got from ponds, dried and dipped in course grease, held in a pair of pincers mounted on a block of wood, were our only means of light; as faggots and cordwood were our only means of heat; and the tinder-box, with its tedious flick, flick, flick, our only means of ignition.

My first sight of the old Town of Horsham, in most of its features and buildings, presented me with a very different picture to that of to-day, and many of the old customs and manners of that time, as well as ninety-nine out of every hundred of the 2,700 people then living in the Town, have disappeared entirely. The ground plan of the old Borough and Town still exists, almost unaltered, within the present Urban District area, and the Causeway, the Bishopric, and here and there in other parts a single house, or perhaps two or three houses together, remain much as they were, but the Streets now hardly seem the same. All the shops were low pitched, very little attempt at display of goods was made in the small windows, all fitted with small panes of glass. Some few tradesmen "illuminated" at night, but only with tallow dips or rushlights. The doors were mostly divided laterally in halves. Some, the more modern, were divided vertically, a few, later, had glass in the upper portions, but as yet there was not a bit of plate glass in the town.

Tradesmen did not keep a large amount of ready-made goods on sale in their shops. Most of them were master craftsmen actually at work with their men upon goods ordered, or substantial necessities; proud of their work, at which they put in many hours, and content to remain active at it till they reached a ripe old age, instead of being mere distributors of other people's productions, as most shopkeepers are to-day. Many trades were flourishing then that are extinct, or nearly so, now. Hats, as well as clothes, chairs and tables, and other household furniture, pattens, baskets, brooms, ropes, spun yarns and twines, leather (as I write I hear the last Horsham Tannery, famous for genuine oak bark tanned sole leather, is just about to close; there used to be four tanyards at Horsham), carriages and harness, saddles and collars, tobacco pipes, baskets, mats, tinware, and other household requisites, all the boots and shoes, leggings and gloves, besides clothes and underwear, were actually manufactured, of course,

EAST STREET, ABOUT 1860.

WEST STREET, ABOUT 1855.

by hand; stocks consisting chiefly of raw material and partly-made goods. Two shop fronts only, Nos. 50 and 51, West Street, are the same now as they were 80 years ago, and nearly every name in the street has changed or vanished, only one remains the same, on the same spot. West Street was then, as now, the principal thoroughfare. I give a list of every tradesman and resident in it about 1830, the houses were then unnumbered, but I commence at the top and go down the names on their respective sides:—

NORTH SIDE.	SOUTH SIDE.
Medwin, lawyer	Knight, tailor
Ireland, Miss, fancy shop	Stanford, draper
Aldridge, W., painter	Lintott, butcher
Washer, bootmaker	Lintott, private house
Cox, tailor	Humphrey, bootmaker
Uwins, harness maker	Warner, hatter
Millward, Mrs., independent	Thorpe, draper
Pickett, ironmonger	Brown, Mrs., independent
Putland, "Castle Inn"	Knight, grocer
Muzzell, clocksmith	Gilburd, Miss, confectioner
Hunt, printer	Laker, Jos., bootmaker
Sadler, "Swan Inn"	Spratley, fellmonger
Goldsmith, upholsterer	Whitham, stationer, &c.
Henley, corn dealer	Laker, bootmaker
Albery, harness maker	Dower, Mrs., general shop
Sharp, G., corn dealer	Browne, draper
Wood, china shop	Bromley, clocksmith
Millward Bros., grocers	Higgins, currier
Pollard, draper and tinman	Chatfield, confectioner
Richardson, upholsterer	Wood, china shop
Griffiths, Mrs., private	Goodbarn, chemist
Tanner, barber	Lintott, Misses, private
Pickett, wood-turner	Turner, wood-turner
Sayers, baker	Chambers, butcher
Boyne, draper	Etherton, ironmonger
Sharp, W., gentleman	Cottington, fruit shop
Smallwood, carpenter	Dendy, corn merchant
Lucas, corn dealer	Burstow, carpenter
Potter, stonemason	Harms & Aldridge, painters
	Murrell, horse dealer
	Robinson, Mrs., "Black Horse"

I give a Map of the Borough and Town of 1831; also a photograph of West Street about 1855, and of East Street about the same date.

Up to 1845 all shops kept open till 9 o'clock p.m. in summer, and 8 o'clock p.m. in winter. After that year, by general agreement, they closed at 8 p.m. in summer, and 7 p.m. in winter. Up to 1836 butchers, bakers, greengrocers, and barbers all kept open shop on Sunday mornings till Church time; butchers' boys on horseback, carrying baskets of meat, galloped round the town on that day as busy as, or busier than, any other day of the week.

One of the most enterprising tradesmen in Horsham was old Johnnie Browne, the draper, who lived at what is now No. 16, West Street. Fashions used not to change so frequently as they do now, but when they did he was the first to have the new ones on sale. He was the first tradesman to sell ready-made boots. He once startled the town by having his name painted in the largest possible sized letters right along the top front of his shop. Just as they were finished, the old man was studying their effect from the opposite side of the street, when a wag asked him " Would you mind lending me a te*legi*oscope; I want to see what letters they are on that building?" " You don't want a te*legi*oscope for *that*," he replied, nettled, " Its a B and a Har and a Ho and a W and a Hen and a He, and that spells Browne," and the old man marched back into his shop.

The Public Houses were centres of social life and intercourse, and of a good deal of drunkenness too. They opened early in the morning, and kept open until late at night—indeed, as often as not, until early the next morning. On Sunday mornings they were open as well, and did a good trade with many who, on account of their previous night's carousal, were possessed of a dry throat. Drinking and gambling went hand in hand, and were very prevalent. The "King's Head," " Anchor," "Black Horse," " Swan,"

"Punch Bowl," "Green Dragon," "Hurst Arms" (which was also known as the "Black Jug"), each of these houses was the favourite of one or other group of tradesmen or others, who used to meet regularly for their business talk and convivial evenings together. Saturday nights were especially convivial. Here is an old song of a later date—1847—expressive of the kind of entertainment enjoyed, and also, it would seem, of a little rivalry between the "Black Jug," kept by Jeremiah Brown, and the King's Head," kept by John Naldrett.

THE SONG OF THE "GO-A-HEADS."

When our week's work is o'er, to the "Jug" we repair,
For we always enjoy ourselves when we meet there,
We laugh, talk, and smoke, and sing with such glee,
No party elsewhere half so happy as we.

Though the swells at the "King's Head" may boast they have got
All the nobs in the town, yet we envy them not,
For no joys are to us like those that are found,
On a Saturday night with our friend Jerry Brown.

When you are thirsty, oh were would you seek,
Such ale and good porter as Jerry Brown keeps;
In our club room for us there's a bright roaring fire,
And to make us all happy it is his desire.

Our number already is over two score,
And before Xmas comes we shall get many more,
For all those that love to hear music's sweet sounds,
Must join the "go-a-heads" when they meet at J. Brown's.

The "King's Head" swells brag about what they can do,
With their pianoforte and their songs that are new;
But we have a "brick," the guitar well can play,
Who can beat all their lot let them try when they may.

For drinking too much we are sometimes to blame,
You may go to the "King's Head" and tell them the same,
There's many a "cove" there, that drinks more I'll be bound
Than any of us or our friend Jerry Brown.

I give a list of the Public Houses and their several landlords about 1830-35: "King's Head," corner of East Street, Mrs. Howe; "Anchor," Market Square, Mr. Lee; "Black Horse," bottom corner of West Street, Mrs. Robinson; "Crown," Carfax, Mr. Bartlett; "Swan," West Street, Mr. Stanford; "Dragon,"

Bishopric, Mr. Scott; "Queen's Head," East Street, Mr. Waters; "Punch Bowl," Middle Street, Mrs. Briggs; "Hurst Arms" or "Black Jug," North Street, Mr. Piper; "Castle," West Street, Mr. Putland; "Lamb," Carfax, Mr. Gardner; "Red Lion," Carfax, Mr. Jas. Lee; "Dog and Bacon," London Road, Mr. Potter.

The "Lamb Inn" at this time used to be at the West corner of Richmond Terrace, where Messrs. King & Chasemore's offices now are. The name of the "Lamb" was afterwards taken by the public house still known as the "Lamb," on the Carfax. This house was hitherto known as the "Red Lion." The old "Lamb" then became the "Richmond" Hotel, with a painted sign of the Richmond Arms on the corner of the house. This hotel then moved to where the Post Office now stands, about the middle of Richmond Terrace. The same sign was put in a frame on a high post opposite on the other side of the road, and the old "Lamb" became a private residence. The "Horse and Groom" was opened about 1844, and the "Railway Inn" soon after the Railway was opened in 1848. The opening of a new public house, or a change of landlord, was always the occasion of a ceremonious dinner and a convivial evening, at which one of the doctors or lawyers or principal tradesmen would preside.

The Post Office I can remember in nine different positions. The first was the south-west corner of Pump Alley, thence it moved to the house right in the corner south-east of the Town Hall, afterwards in succession to what is now 19, Market Square, 11, West Street; 54, West Street; 48, West Street; 4, West Street; 31, Carfax; 16, Carfax (its present position); and I have known of eight Postmasters in succession, viz., Messrs. Elphick senior and junior,

Tugwell, Breads, Price, Goldsmith, Poole, and the present one, Mr. Clarke.

I also give the names of the larger private houses in the neighbourhood, and the names of their residents: Horsham Park, R. Hurst, Esq. (M.P. for Horsham, 1812-29); Causeway House, R. H. Hurst, Esq., son (M.P. for Horsham, 1832-41 and 1843-47); Manor House, N. Tredcroft, Esq.; Denne Park, — Platt, Esq.; Field Place, Sir T. Shelley; Strood, Admiral Commerell; Holbrook, Sir Jas. Whitshed; Chestnut Lodge, B. Fox, Esq.; Tanbridge, Miss Wolff; Tanfield, Mrs. Marriott; Millmeades, — Watkyns, Esq.; Springfield, Mr. Thornton; New Lodge, R. Aldridge, Esq.; Nunnery, T. Sanctuary, Esq.; Lyne, J. Broadwood, Esq.; Holmbush, T. Broadwood, Esq.; Leonardslee, Colonel Beauclerc; Muntham, — Chitty, Esq.; Coolhurst, Marchioness of Northampton; Knepp, Sir C. Burrell.

The roads in the town and neighbourhood were very bad in winter. There was no steam-roller for road-making or repairing. Flints were put down, usually at the end of the autumn, where thought to be wanted, and gradually worked in by the traffic. The country bye-roads were, of course, worse, and frequently quite impassable. Up to about 1840 turnpike roads only were hard. Like other people, my father, in travelling round the country roads, would sometimes find the wheels of his cart sunk in the mud up to the boxes, and be forced to borrow a farmer's horse to pull them out. Waggons always carried a spade for scraping the wheels, which, coming from a bye-road to the turnpike road, would sometimes be covered and filled in with clay or mud, looking like mill-stones. Sometimes it would take nine or ten horses to get a loaded waggon out of a bad road or up a steep hill. Even as late as 1851 I have sometimes found it impossible to walk to Newdigate without sinking in the mud nearly up to the calf of my leg. The pavements or causeways of the town, too, were but very indifferently laid and maintained; not that the town was unable to pave its street well had the authorities chosen to do so, for Horsham stone was plentiful and famous for roofing and paving. It was quarried in large quantities, but shoemakers always go the worst shod; Horsham sent most of its stone—and that the best—away to other places.

The amount of vehicular traffic through the town was considerable, though of course not to be compared to that of to-day, and not sufficient even in West Street to prevent us boys playing marbles there. Several four-horse coaches, to and from London, Brighton, Worthing, Oxford, Reading, and Windsor passed through the town daily, calling at the " King's Head," " Anchor," and " Crown." In 1833 Horsham started its own direct London Coach, " The Star," which set out from the " Swan," in West Street, every morning except Sunday all the year round, at 7 a.m. punctually; reached the " Old Bell Inn," Holborn, at 11.45 a.m., started the return journey at 3.15 p.m., and arrived back at the Swan at 8 p.m. Little Bob Whittle, the coachman, who lived in the Causeway, was a thorough artist on the box. He was reputed to be the prettiest driver and whip and altogether the smartest coachman that drove into London. 'Twas said he could whip a fly off one of the leading horses nose without touching the horse. Poor Bob; his customers gradually deserted his horse for the steam engine: traps began running from Horsham to Three Bridges Station, whence the journey to and from London by train was quicker and cheaper. A pair horse 'bus ran regularly from Pulborough through Horsham to Three Bridges and back, picking up some of his customers. Many old people stuck to the turnpike, and vowed they would never get into a railway train; among these was my father; but eventually poor Bob found his occupation gone. In 1846, when but 41 years of age, he took ill and died, 'twas said of a broken heart. Old Lloyd, the carrier, who lived at the corner of Wickersham's Lane, then called Lloyd's Yard, suffered a similar fate. He continued his journeys, with his four-horse waggons, to London as long as he could, but the goods he used to carry, via Dorking, transferred to the Three Bridges road, and when Horsham Station was built he found the ground taken, as it were, from under him. Post chaises, too, swifter and more expensive means of travel (2s. per mile was their regular price), to and from almost everywhere, came through the town, in addition to those that plied for hire, kept at the above Hotels. Now and again the private four-horse coaches and chaises of the large-landed gentry would travel through, whilst the private carriages and chaises of the local gentry went about daily, visiting or shopping. Many four-horse, and sometimes six-horse, farmers and carriers' waggons, laden with corn, barley, coal, timber, stone, groceries, and many other commodities, some fetching their loads from the Canal at West Grinstead, some from that at Newbridge, Billingshurst, more than equalled in bulk the other kinds of traffic, to which must be added that of the many farmers, professional gentlemen, and tradesmen who rode horseback; of the few yoked oxen going along very steadily and very, very slowly, and of the many dog carts that were in vogue for some years. The dogs were usually harnessed three-a-breast to small low-built carts. Several rural postmen went their rounds in them, and many hawkers of fish drove up here from Worthing and Brighton. The dogs travelled very fast, especially at starting, and barked loudly as they went along. A man named Whiting owned the fastest dogs in Horsham, but he was very cruel to them, and was one day made to apologise to them by a magistrate, under threat of prosecution. In fact the dogs were generally ill-used and, partly in consequence, this mode of travel was legally abolished in 1854.

Almost as soon as I could toddle I was sent to an infant school — the first infant school opened at Horsham. It was kept by Miss Jane Sayers, in the west end of the old barn still standing on the south side of the Bishopric, nearly opposite our house. My first year's schooling was paid for by a generous old quaker, Mr. Pollard, who then lived at " The Druids." Very little was done in those days to make schools attractive, but I enjoyed myself the short time I was with Miss Sayers, who looked upon me as an apt pupil. Every day we used to sing " God save George, our King," until his death in 1830, when I well remember Miss Sayers saying to us, "You must not sing George any more, it's William now." Miss Sayers soon after moved to Springfield Road, then called Chapel Lane, and joined the British Schools at the north end of London Road; here I stayed till 1834, helping mother between my school hours trim pipes, for which she used to get 3d. per gross. In 1834 I went to the Church School, then held in Hill's Chancel, in the north side of the Church, occasionally having a day off to help old Albery, the harness maker, make ropes at his ropewalk from the corner of the Bishopric along the west side of Springfield Road, for which he paid me 6d. per day. In 1838 I " got in " to Collyer's Free School, where I stayed until it was pulled down in 1840. I give a reproduction of a painting of the old school by myself in 1838.

In 1840 I was apprenticed to Jim Vaughan, who lived in the Causeway, to learn the boot and shoe-making trade. At a time when as yet there were no boot-making machines, and no ready-made boots,

COLLYER'S SCHOOL, 1540—1840.

boot making was quite an important local industry; I daresay there were forty or fifty men regularly employed at it in Horsham. They were called cord-wainers, or snobs, and were good hard-workers and sound beer-drinkers to a man. Indeed, so notorious were they as drinkers that when I went into the trade my mother's friends said to her, "Ah! Harry's done for now." But I can truthfully say that, though I stuck to the trade for the whole of my life, I took neither to "drinking" nor smoking; the only time I was ever drunk was once when I was the victim of a conspiracy to make me so. The first year I worked without getting payment; the next year I was paid 2s. per week, rising 1s. per week at the end of each year until I was out of my time. I stayed with Mr. Vaughan about ten years, and then went to work for Mr. Gilburd, in Middle Street, then called Butcher's Row, and was almost entirely employed by him at making women's boots, for which I was paid at first 1s. 4d. per pair, afterwards 1s. 6d. per pair. With Mr. Gilburd I stayed 30 years, till he died in 1880. On an average I earned perhaps 15s. per week, cer-tainly not more, for a week's work of 60 to 70 hours. The greatest number of pairs of boots I ever made in one week was 13, thereby earning 19s. 6d.; that week I worked every available hour, and did nothing else except eat, drink, and sleep. I never once took 20s. for a week's work at my trade, so the reader can understand I never made enough money to warp my political convictions, and do not possess enough to worry about now, as after a life's hard work I stand at the brink of the grave.

The first event outside our house that I have any recollection of was the last night funeral at Horsham, which took place in November, 1829, when Mrs. Killick, from Tanbridge, was buried. These night funerals were elaborate, ceremonious affairs, with

torch-light procession, accorded only to the rich. I
was not present on this occasion; my recollections
are but second hand, derived from hearing my
brothers and sisters talking about it the next morning.
Another remarkable night funeral I have heard my
father say was that of Miss Elizabeth Gatford, a
most eccentric lady, who died the 8th July, 1799.
She willed, in 1790, that her corpse was not to be
buried for one month, and that spirits of wine was
to be used for its preservation. Accordingly between
£30 and £40 was spent in this manner; she also
willed that she was to be buried in four coffins—a
shell, and one each of lead, oak, and stone, and
that the ceremony should not take place until after
10 o'clock at night. She was buried in a vault at
the Old Baptist Chapel, in Worthing Road, at 12
o'clock mid-night, the Rev. Evans, of Worship
Street, London, preaching the burial sermon. The
chapel and burial ground were crowded with church
folk and dissenters of all sects. In her will she left
£15 per annum to support, till they died, certain
animals, cats, dogs, parrots, guinea pigs, &c., whom
she had lived with; and also £5 5s. per annum to be
given in bread to the poor, a charitable bequest that
is still regularly discharged.

I can also recollect hearing my brothers and sisters
talking of a murder committed on Saturday, 8th
March, 1830, at the " Queen's Head " Inn. Several
young men were inside that house drinking and card
playing, when, late at night, they fell out among
themselves. The landlord turned them outside, when
two of them, Harry Hewett and Edward Smith
resumed the quarrel. After fighting a few minutes,
Hewitt took out a knife and stabbed Smith, who died
in consequence after about a quarter of an hour. In
the small crowd round the two fighters were Hewett's
mother, Charlotte Venn, and brother. The mother

egged her son on to fight, "give it to him, Harry,"
she cried, "have your revenge;" but the brother
tried to get the knife away, and in doing so had his
hand cut very badly. Hewett was lodged in Horsham
Goal to await his trial at the coming Horsham
Assizes. The following verses were written on the
occasion, and used to be sung about the town :—

> At the "Queen's Head" Inn in Horsham Town,
> Poor Edward Smith met his death wound;
> Drinking and gaming, and playing at cards,
> Causes the best of friends to have words.
>
> Drinking and gaming till twelve at night,
> Then out in the street they went to fight;
> Poor Smith thought he'd a friend so nigh,
> But proved to be an enemy.
>
> Young Hewett with his knife so sharp,
> Aimed several times at poor Smith's heart,
> He gave one stab, such a horrid deed,
> Enough to make one's heart to bleed.
>
> What could a mother be thinking on,
> To stand near by and see her son
> Engage in wicked, deadly, strife,
> And rob his poor young friend of life.
>
> The Horsham Assizes now draw near,
> And at the bar Hewett must appear:
> Before the Judge he now must stand,
> With aching heart and trembling hand.
>
> Young men! take warning by his plight,
> Shun drink and cards by day and night,
> Be honest, sober, kind, and free,
> And so avoid such misery.

At the last Horsham Assizes, held on the 30th March,
1830, the charge of murder was preferred, but Hewett
was found guilty of manslaughter only. He was
sentenced to transportation to Bermuda for life, but
came back to Horsham after the expiration of ten
years of his sentence.

I can just remember the Coronation of King
William IV., Thursday, Sept. 15th, 1831. It was a
general holiday, and the occasion of great festivities.
The celebration here commenced with the ringing of
the Church bells, which continued on and off all day.

There was a procession round the town, headed by the band, in the afternoon, and a public dinner at the King's Head Hotel in the evening.

The celebration was somewhat overshadowed by the prevailing political conditions and was quite eclipsed by the Reform dinner and festivities which took place on Wednesday, the 1st August, 1832, to celebrate the passing of the Reform Bill. I was present with my elder brother at these festivities, and can recall particulars of the event, as if they took place but last week. The morning was ushered in by a peal of bells from the old Church, the band afterwards playing round the town. Towards noon throngs of people from all quarters entered the town, on foot and in vehicles of all kinds. At 2 o'clock the people assembled in four different parts of the town, the parties distinguished from one another by different colours; pink, green, yellow, or white, and marched to the Carfax, whence, headed by the band, all marched to the Cricket Field, which was then in the North Parade, just south of where Hurst Road is now. By about 3.30 p.m. the whole company, nearly 3000 people, were seated at 62 tables, loaded with cold roast and boiled beef and mutton, vegetables, hot plum pudding, and beer. A special platform was erected for the chairman, T. Sanctuary, Esq., late High Sheriff of Sussex, and his supporters. At the sound of a bugle grace was said before and after the dinner. There were all kinds of sports and amusements, races, &c., until about 6 o'clock in the evening, when, unfortunately, it came on to rain hard, and my brother then carried me home on his back. The day closed with a brilliant display of fireworks; rockets, candles, vertical wheels, mines, balloons, Bengal lights, jacks-in-boxes, maroons, tourbillions, &c., &c. About 4,000 people altogether were present at the Cricket Field. In the evening there was a grand ball at the King's

Head Hotel. A second and third display of fireworks took place in the evenings of the two succeeding days.

This happy event, however, took place in very troublous times. The country, generally, was in a very unsettled state, and in the neighbourhood of Horsham, as elsewhere, there was a great amount of agricultural distress and rioting, no less than five young men were hanged here between 1831 and 1834 for rick firing at various places in Sussex. There were further disturbances about 1834-5 upon the introduction of the new Poor Law, which was very unpopular with the labouring classes. The magistrates, unable to maintain order through the constables, frequently sent to Brighton for a troop of cavalry to do so. These soldiers were usually billetted here for several weeks together. Their presence in the town at this time, when the spirit of " Reform " was in the air and demands for greater liberties and privileges were being made by all workers, was very irritating to our parents ; but from a spectacular point of view was very satisfactory to us boys. I can see them now, one captain, one lieutenant, one sergeant, two corporals, and usually about twenty-five troopers, marching round the town ; sometimes they would pass down the Bishopric to Broadbridge Heath Common for drill and sword exercise. Our limited vision apprehended nothing but their outward prettiness, and our sympathies were entirely with the soldiers, who in their smart uniforms, with their bright swords and prancing horses, all untouched by the grinding industrial conditions of the time, compared but too favourably with the poor labourers, who in their poverty were taxed and sweated for the soldiers upkeep.

In former days the labourers were all called happy men,
As well they might be ; labourers could keep a grunter then ;
But in these days a grunter is but a poor man lent—
Hard times—now he must kill and sell his pig to pay the rent.

Before the new Union Workhouse was built, in 1838, through the operation of the new Poor Law, Horsham Parish Workhouse was in the Normandy, where the Alms Houses are now. There, some of the disturbances above alluded to took place, and the magistrates in a body were once mobbed and pelted with stones by the angry labourers. A dismal kind of place, too, where the mad as well as the poor were kept. I have heard of two mad people kept there, one a man named Evans, a raving maniac, who occupied one cell for 22 years, and was released only by grim death. He was succeeded in the same cell by his daughter, who was there in chains, also for many years; I don't know how many. She was kept, as it were, on show, visitors being allowed to look at her through iron bars in the door, and watch her cultivating the friendship of rats—rats of enormous size, which she used to nurse in her lap and feed from her hands. Upon the slightest noise by visitors the rats would disappear leaving the poor maniac convulsed with rage and uttering the most awful imprecations upon their disturbers.

I can well remember the Parliamentary Election, the "Reform" election as it was called, of 1832. Against Mr. Hurst, the popular Horsham candidate, the Duke of Norfolk ran his auditor, Mr. Blount, but the town soon showed it resented the Duke's political interference. Early on polling day his candidate, finding he had no chance of winning, gave up the contest. Soon afterwards, not knowing this, a party of his supporters, with band playing and colours flying, paraded the town. As they came down the Bishopric my father, with whom I was standing at the door of our cottage, cried out to them, in glee, "Ha! Ha! Blount has given up, you're done as brown as bricks." There was a great amount of drunkenness at this and the following elections; Public Houses were "open" and drinks were "free." But by far the greatest amount of drunkenness at any election in my time took place at that of 1847—one of the most notoriously drunken and corrupt elections in the United Kingdom. "Free" liquor could be had at every public house and beer shop in the parish for several weeks. The consequence was, that whilst some people kept sober others were continually drunk, and many others were continuously ditto. On nomination and polling days it may almost be said the town was entirely drunk. The bribery was almost as bad as the drunkenness; many "free and independent" citizens were bribed for their vote, others were bribed not to vote. Others again were kidnapped away so that they could not vote. A platform, called the Hustings, was erected against the Town Hall, and here the candidates and friends and the returning officer assembled on nomination day for the purpose of nominating the candidates, and on the following day—election day— to receive votes, which used to be given openly by word of mouth, not by ballot. A feature of old time electioneering at Horsham were the "white boys," of whom, in 1847, I was one. Each candidate had about twenty. Each white boy was dressed in a white round frock and carried a pole about six feet long, painted red or blue, according to the colour favoured by the candidate in whose interests he was engaged. We were paid 5s. each per day, and we could have as much to eat and drink as we liked. Our duties were to keep the way to the hustings clear for voters, and to make ourselves otherwise generally useful. Polling ceased punctually at 4 p.m., but the member who won in 1847 found himself in a very shaky seat indeed. A petition against his return was lodged, and so flagrant had been the conduct of the election by his supporters

that it was found he had not a leg to stand, or rather
sit, upon. No defence was made, and he was unseated. This verdict had the effect of sobering the
town, for the subsequent election, in 1848, was per-
fectly tame and respectably conducted. The defeated
candidate of 1847 again put up, and was this time
elected by a large majority over his new opponent;
but he was not allowed to take his seat; a petition
against his return was lodged for exactly the same
offences, and at the same election as that upon which
he had petitioned against his former rival, and he was
also unseated. There had been enough drunkenness
in 1847 to unseat fifty members of Parliament; but
there has never been anything approaching it at any
election at Horsham since.

On Sunday, Mar. 31st, 1833, there was felt, all over
the Town, quite a severe shock of earthquake. It
took place at a quiet time, about 8.30 p.m., when
most people were sitting at home, and everybody
was greatly alarmed. Housebells started ringing of
themselves, scales were put in motion, and pictures
swung on the walls; people ran out of their houses
fearing the beams would give way and apprehensive
of the safety of themselves and their goods. Fortunately no serious damage was done, and no further
shock was felt.

On Thursday, Sept. 15th, 1835, I went to see the
horse racing that then took place in St. Leonard's
Forest. The first race meeting held there, in 1834,
was rather small, but met with much encouragement
and success. The '35 meeting was quite a grand
event: early in the morning every approach to the
Forest was crowded with vehicles of all kinds, and
with people on foot and on horseback. By 10 o'clock,
the hour at which the first race was timed to start,
it was estimated that quite 12,000 people and 1,000
horses were present. It was said that these races

attracted more people to the neighbourhood of Horsham than any other event ever did. The day was beautifully fine and the races were run in a delightful spot. The course, one-and-a-half miles in circumference, was on the west side of the big house, New Lodge. I climbed up a tree and had a full view of the whole day's proceedings, of which I give a programme.

ST. LEONARD'S FOREST RACES,

On Tuesday, Sept. 15th, 1835,

At ten o'clock precisely.

A Saddle and Bridle for Ponies under 13 hands.

The last half mile.

Master Smith's gr. g. "Speculation," yellow and black stripes, black cap

Mr. Trowers' bl. m. "Deception," yellow body, black cap   1

Mr. Lee's br. m. "Fanny," white, black cap

Mr. Geo. Sharp's br. g. "Hazard," scarlet, black cap

Mr. Oakes' br. g. "Bounce," blue body, black cap

Mr. Bartlett's br. g. "XXX," pink body, white sleeves, green and yellow cap

Mr. Thomas' b. m. "Lady Hamilton," blue, white cap   2

The Victuallers' Cup and Sweepstakes.

For Horses not thorough bred, nor exceeding 14 hands 3in.

One mile and a distance.

Mr. Martin's bl. g. "Willie Wilkin," aged, 12st, pink body, green sleeves, black cap   2

Mr. Rickword's gr. m. "Mermaid," 5 yrs., 11st., green, black cap   1

Mr. Redford's br. m. "Brown Bess," aged, 12st., crimson, black cap   3

Mr. Chasemore's b. m. "Chance," aged, white, black cap

Mr. Rawlison's b. g. "Maplehurst," 4 yrs., 10st., crimson and black stripe, black cap

The Town Cup and Sweepstakes.

For Horses not thorough bred. Two miles and a distance.

Mr. Coppard's gr. m. "Miss Peggy," 4 yrs., 10st. 10lbs., crimson and black stripes, black cap   2

Mr. Howes' b. m. "Lilley of the Valley," 4 yrs., 10st. 10lbs., green body, white sleeves, white cap   1

Mr. Lee's b. g. "Fencer," 4 yrs., 10st. 10lbs., white, black cap

The Ladies' purse of thirty sovereigns, added to a subscription of £5 each.

Two miles and a distance.

The owner of the second horse to receive back his stake.

Mr. Platt's gr. m. "My Lady" (by Skim), 6 yrs., 12st., light blue jacket, blue stripe cap   3

Mr. Redford's br. m. "Brown Bess," aged, 11st. 6lbs., crimson, black cap

Mr. Bazelgette's gr. g. "Spicy," aged, 13st., white, black cap   1

Mr. Padwick's b. g. "Roadster," aged, 11st. 6lb., lilac, black cap   2

The Hunters' Sweepstakes and purse. For horses not thorough bred, belonging to gentlemen who have regularly hunted with Mr. Steere's hounds.

Two miles and a distance.

The owner of the second horse to receive back his stake.

Mr. Platt's gr. m. "My Lady" (by Skim), 6 yrs., 12st., light blue jacket, blue stripe cap

Mr. Sanctuary's gr. m. "The Lady Abbess" (by Little John), 5 yrs., 11st. 6lbs., orange, black cap

Mr. Martin's gr. m. "Fair Maid" (by Acu Punctu), 6 yrs., 12st., pink body, green sleeves, black cap   2

Mr. Coppard's gr. m. "Miss Peggy" (by Acu Punctu), 4 yrs., 10st., crimson and black striped, black cap

Mr. Aldridge's ns. br. g. "Accommodation," 7 yrs., 12st. 2lbs., crimson, black cap   1

Mr. Lee Steere's ns. b. m. "Lilly of the Valley," 4 yrs., 10st. 10lbs., green body, white sleeves, white cap

Mr. Lee's b. g. "Fencer," 4 yrs., 10st. 10lbs., white, black cap

The Yeomanry Cup, presented by H. D. Goring, Esq., M.P., for horses belonging to the Arundel and Bramber Yeomanry.

To carry 12st. each. One mile and a distance.

Mr. G. Penfold's ch. h. "Wiggenholt," aged, pink body, white sleeves, pink cap   1

Mr. G. Duke's m. "Hope," aged, pink body, blue sleeves, black cap

Mr. R. Watkyns' h. "Bobino," aged, green body, pink sleeve, black cap   3

Mr. Cook's "Arundel"

Any winner of a previous cup or stakes to carry 6lbs. extra.

JOHN SHELLEY, Esq.,
LEE STEERE, Esq.,
ROBERT ALDRIDGE, Esq.,
G. E. PLATT, Esq.,
} Stewards.

There was a race ball and supper in the evening at the King's Head Hotel.

These race meetings were held annually for seven years. I never attended any others, but I got enough experience to warn me of their attendant evils— betting, drinking, and swindling. Refreshments of all kinds were on sale or, I should perhaps say, were sold, for some of the more enthusiastic supporters of the turf were carried off the ground on hurdles.

At the 1836 race meeting a big bazaar was held on the course to raise money for building the little Church in the Coolhurst grounds. I am unable to define the bonds of sympathy between the racecourse and the Church, but they were strong enough to raise over £200 at this bazaar. On the other hand they were very offensive to the popular Horsham curate, Mr. Kenrick, whose representations to the owner of St. Leonard's as to the presence of so many undesirable characters, hawks and pigeons, sharps and flats, bounders, boozers, and harpies of all sorts at the races, brought about their discontinuance.

The most important sporting event at Horsham, previous to these races, that I ever heard of, took place in 1823, when a man named Verrall, called the " Lad," undertook to walk 1000 miles in 20 consecutive days for a wager of £30. Verrall, 43 years of age, married, with 11 children, a pig jobber by trade, had fallen upon hard times and decided to try the sporting instincts of the Town as a means of improving his fortunes. His walk was from the " Swan " Inn to the " Dog and Bacon " Inn and back again, a distance of exactly a mile each way, twenty-five times daily, fifty miles a day. He started on Tuesday, Nov. 4th, 1823, at 4.30 a.m., and finished his first day's work just after 9 p.m. The next day he started at 4 a.m. and finished at 7 p.m. ; on Thursday he started at 4.30 a.m. and finished 9.30 p.m. He declared "The lad will not give in until he can go no longer, and of that he is not afraid." He had had no previous training except the walking from town to town necessitated by his ordinary business. His attempt at such a record met with a great amount of support in the Town. The people on the coaches, too, were very interested and also encouraged him. He stuck to his self-imposed task and manfully completed it within the specified time, though he got so sleepy towards the end that he was obliged to have a man to support him and keep him awake. He finished on the night of Sunday, Nov. 24th, the old Band playing him in at the finish, thus winning his wager and making altogether in winnings and presents £300.

Horsham was first lighted by gas on Monday, Jan. 25th, 1836. It cannot be said the lighting of the town previously was very brilliant. The few oil lamps about the streets were kept more or less in bad order and odour by old Tinker Smith, and there were besides a few more, one each attached to several private houses; nor can it now be said the new illuminant was very brilliant either, but it was thought to be so ; my own expectations ran very high. " Ah," I had heard it said, " this new gas is something wonderful ; it beats all your common daylight." On the first night of lighting up by the new way the streets were crowded with folk, many of whom came in from the country to enjoy the sensation. At the "King's Head" Hotel there was a large-sized star of gas jets ; at the "Crown" Inn there was a large crown produced in the same way. The Town Hall decoration, consisting of a large W.R. with jets around, compelled everyone's admiration. Standing by me an old countryman asked his neighbour, " What does W.R. mean ? " " W stands for William and R for Rex," replied the individual addressed. " What does Rex mean, then," persisted the yokel : " Oh, that means God Almighty bless him," was the further answer, which seemed quite satisfactory. The price of gas at first was 12s. 6d. per 1000 ft.; in 1848 it was reduced to 10s. per 1000 ft.

On Tuesday, the 29th Nov., 1836, there raged the most tremendous storm that ever happened in my life; the wind began to rise in the morning and gradually gained in strength till about 12 o'clock noon, when it had acquired a terrific force. We schoolboys, and the Collyer's school boys, got a lot of fun out of it; we went round the south side of the Church and when we got to the Belfry door, we spread out our jackets like sails, and were irresistibly carried up to the Churchyard gates by the wind, which blew from the S.W. It was impossible for us to go back the way we came, so we went round the East end of the Church to get into position and repeat the fun; this we did many times. As we went up the Causeway and into the streets things began to look and sound very serious. I got home to dinner just about 1 o'clock, and we had but just sat down to it when Mother cried out, alarmed, "Did you hear that hallooing?" "No," we replied, for the wind was making such a noise that we had heard no voices. "A house has blown down with someone in it!" she said, in an agitated voice. I rushed out to see if she spoke truly and, surely enough, a few doors off, a cottage had been completely wrecked; nothing of it was left standing but the chimney stack. Mrs. Smith, who lived there (mother of the lad who was killed at the "Queen's Head"), luckily escaped death or mutilation through having gone to the door to see if her husband was returning to dinner, and there she stood, unhurt, just where her doorway used to be. Mrs. Grinstead, an old lodger, who was quietly sitting upstairs, was almost as fortunate: when the floor gave way, she, bed, bedding, and all else crashed down, but she got nothing worse than a shaking. I can plainly see her now, quite dazed, supported by a few neighbours, all standing in the middle of the wreck. As soon as she collected her wits, she philosophically applied them to the situation. "It's nobody's fault," she said, addressing the small crowd, "it must be a ' Poor Law ' wind," referring to the then new and unpopular poor law. Everything possessed by the occupants was destroyed, and a fund was immediately raised in the Town to replace them. As we stood there an old man, Harry Fillary, brought us news of further havoc up Town. "This ! !" he cried, contemplating the scene, "this is nothing, just go up Town and see the houses ! Why, Dr. Martin's stables have all blown down atop of the horses." I went up Town and, though old Harry had exaggerated somewhat, things were bad enough, surely : very few houses or buildings had been able to completely withstand the fury of the storm. Both chimneys of Dr. Martin's house had blown down and one had crashed into the stable. The Independent, or, as it was then called, Harms' Chapel, was almost entirely unroofed ; slates blew off houses by the score ; the streets were strewn with chimney pots, bricks, and all sorts of debris ; slates and tiles went flying about in all directions, to the consternation of everybody. It seemed just as if some unseen giant hand were stripping the houses of their roofs and hurling the dangerous missiles about regardless of everything. Outside the Town trees were dismembered and uprooted by the score, by the hundred. Some of the finest elm trees round the Barrack walks were ruined : eight or ten in Spring-field Park were blown right across the North Parade. Denne Park also suffered much, whilst Mick Mills' race, which seemed to lay right in the track of the wind, was completely denuded of mature growing timber; only young saplings that could bend to the violence of the storm were left standing. Upwards of 1500 full-grown trees were here "dashed down and scattered by the winds assiduous fury." The mansion and outbuildings at St. Leonard's also received great injury, whilst everywhere cornstacks and hayricks, barns and hovels, were unroofed and scattered like chaff. The storm lasted till late in the evening, when we began to hear of the mischief it had done in many other places. The next morning we heard it had blown down Brighton Chain Pier.

I have heard my father speak of storms in his time, before I was born, one particularly in 1790 when the Church steeple was struck by lightning and set on fire; the fire was soon extinguished by the rain, which fell in torrents. It was soon after this that a lightning conductor was first fixed to the steeple. Again, on Tuesday, the 28th March, 1809, there was a very severe storm, and such an amount of rain as literally to flood the town; and on Sunday, the 1st July, 1810, a yet worse storm broke over the town and did much damage.

The coldest weather I ever remember came in at the beginning of 1838. The extraordinary severity of it was first remarked upon on Sunday, 14th January, when the thermometer fell to zero; grape and elderberry wine was frozen solid. The cold continued to increase till Saturday, the 20th January, when the thermometer fell to 16 degrees below zero. "The cold was so intense as never before to have been "felt by anyone living, and caused a peculiar feeling "impossible to describe. Gin was now also found to "be frozen solid. Innumerable small icicles or thin "wedges of ice were noticed floating in the air, and "glistened like prisms as the sun shone on them.*"

---

* See letter in "West Sussex County Times," Jan. 9th, 1909, by Mr. Honeywood.

I remember coming down to breakfast on this particular morning, we hugged the fire pretty closely. When we had finished breakfast we found the cups were frozen to the saucers. I heard too, afterwards, that some of the carter boys' noses had frozen as they came in to the Horsham market.

On Thursday, 29th November, the same year, there was a very severe hailstorm, the most severe one yet remembered, which did a lot of damage, but it was quite eclipsed on the 7th of July, 1839, when in a short space of time many hundreds of pounds worth of glass was smashed, besides incalculable other damage done. Fortunately, it happened on a Sunday evening, between 8 and 9 o'clock, when all the shops and many private houses had their shutters up. The storm, with much thunder and lightning, came on rather suddenly. Some of the hailstones, rough and jagged, were as large as walnuts, and tore peoples umbrellas to ribbons. Every skylight in the town, and all the glass in the gardens of the large houses in the neighbourhood was smashed to atoms. The damage at Lyne was £500, at Holbrook £200, at Denne £150, at Tanbridge £60; nearly everybody suffered more or less, and whilst the storm lasted everybody was frightened. The glaziers only were in a contented frame of mind; one of them, indeed, received an inspiration, by breakfast time he had cornered all the glass in the town, with which he immediately set about repairing yesterday's havoc, the others having to wait for fresh supplies from London, then fetched by old Jas. Lloyd the carrier, a matter of three or four days.

On Wednesday, the 23rd August, 1837, there was a big jewel robbery, the largest of its kind known at Horsham. During the night thieves broke into Michael Bromley's shop and stole £300 worth of the best of his stock. The attack was deliberately planned and successfully carried out by persons who knew their business : they took all the gold and silver articles and went their way undiscovered, leaving old Michael to get what satisfaction he might out of the plated goods they had disdainfully rejected.

On Thursday, the 13th February, 1840, there was another big robbery in West Street, this time at Messrs. Henty's Bank. In the first two or three decades of the 19th century Horsham was noted for the frequency of its bank failures. No other town of its size suffered more from theirs. In this chronic state of insolvency they were thought, I suppose, by respectable burglars not worthy of attack ; anyhow, I never before heard of a bank robbery in the town, but in 1840 there seemed to appear the prospect of a good haul. It was supposed the thieves concealed themselves in the bank a day or two. On the night of the robbery the keys of the strong room were taken from under the Bank Manager's head as he lay asleep, and £450 in hard cash was taken by the thieves, who, after regaling themselves with ham and wine, got safely away with their booty, and were never again heard of.

Lots of people in my time mistrusted the banks, and would not put their money in them. I heard of an old farmer at Shipley who, having been warned by his doctor that he had not long to live, sent for his two sons and told them that he had £600 in cash hidden in the pigeon coo, and that when he was dead they were to divide it. The old man, however, notwithstanding the doctor's warning and medicines, got better—got quite well. When he went to the pigeon coo he found it empty, an experience that probably bred as great a mistrust of his sons as that he had of the banks.

Then there were old Jack and Will Weller, who lived up Hurst Hill, they were reputed to be worth a lot of money. One day old Jack came into the shop of Mr. Gilburd, my master, with a pocket full of gold, between £80 and £100. Mr. Gilburd said to him, "You old silly, why don't you put the money in the Bank?" "Bank, be —," he replied, "I can keep it a — sight better myself," a statement he was soon after able to prove, for he and his brother were late at night visited by four or five roughs: "What do you want," asked Jack; "What we can get," they replied, "and we mean to have it." "Do you by —, then we must see what we can do." Jack got his gun and bayonet, and the brother a watchman's rattle, and with these they frightened their assailants away.

On the 25th June, 1837, the Windsor Coach brought news of the death of King William IV. to Horsham, and on the following Oct. 5th the new Queen we heard would be travelling by post chaise from London to Brighton, going through Crawley and Peas Pottage. We had heard a lot of talk about the new young Queen, who, I thought, must be something wonderful, so on Oct. 4th about twelve of us Rookery boys ranging in age from eight to fourteen years of age, met, and determined to walk to Peas Pottage to see her go through there; one of the smaller boys, Bill Etheridge, was so poorly dressed, being literally in rags, and without boots at all fit for such a journey, that the other boys threatened he should not go. "What'll the Queen think of him and his tatters?" asked one of the bigger boys contemptuously. The prospect of offending the Queen by his appearance, or of being deprived of the chance of seeing her, made the boy cry; so I made up my mind he should not be disappointed. "Never mind, Bill," I said to him after the others had gone, "you shall see her alright; you and I will start off together early in the morning before the others; I know the way alright." I didn't know the way, but I wanted to pacify him, and I felt sure I could find it. Accordingly, about seven o'clock the next morning, Bill, in nothing but his rags, and I, with nothing more than the clothes I stood up in, started off, trusting to luck to lead us the right way and fill our little bellies. We trudged on alone, through Roffey, hoping for a friendly waggoner to give us a lift, but none came along. At length we got to Pease Pottage, where we saw a large archway made of evergreens, with " VICTORIA REGINA " worked on it in various coloured dahlias ; we were mightily impressed, and felt we must now tread the ground very lightly. Here we waited until the other Horsham Rookery boys came up, when, hearing the Queen's chaise would change horses at Crawley, and thinking we should get a straighter and longer stare at her there, we decided to go. We found Crawley very gaily decorated and crowded with people. All the school children were penned in like sheep, awaiting the Royal arrival, and under orders to sing when called upon. We, the Horsham contingent, now getting very hungry, crowded ourselves together in a bunch close to the " George Hotel," carefully hiding in our midst our ragged and tattered little companion, lest the Queen when she came might see him and, perhaps, we thought, order his head off. Presently the Queen and her mother, in a post chaise, with post boys and outriders, and escorted by a large number of yeomen from the neighbourhood, each carrying a white staff, drove up to the Hotel, close to us boys. The Crawley folk cheered tremendously, but the sight of these two very ordinary-looking women by no means satisfied our youthful but elevated ideas of Royalty; worse ! it did not appease our hunger, now thoroughly aggravated by the information that the Crawley youths were to have a big feed as soon as the Queen was gone. "Which is the Queen, then, Harry?" asked

D

Tom Vinall of me. "Why, the young 'un, I suppose," I answered crossly. I felt disappointed and hungry enough almost to be uncivil, and as the crowd sang "God save the Queen," &c., I could not help thinking He would be attending to a more necessitous case if, instead of "sending her victorious," He sent us Horsham boys something solid to eat, together with a new suit of clothes and a pair of boots for Bill Etheridge. With the Queen gone, the Crawley people dispersing, and without a farthing between us Horsham boys, we had now to face the seven miles' walk home; this we did, luckily finding a few blackberries in the hedges, our only refreshment all day, getting back at night thoroughly exhausted. Many people walked from Horsham to Brighton the same day to see Brighton's welcome to the young Queen. Some of my elder brothers went. Poor Billy Claytor, who was something of a simpleton, decided to go, and having been told he would be able to get nothing to eat at Brighton, provided himself with a gallon loaf of bread, which he carried with him.

Speaking of Royalty, it will surprise most and, I am sure, gratify many of my readers to know that a Royal wedding has actually taken place at Horsham. It is astonishing to me to find how nearly completely this celebrated event has faded from the minds of Horsham people, yet it was thought a lot of, and much talked about, at the time. It was not an ideal wedding—both bride and bridegroom were over 60—and it was said that the prospect of a smooth running of their united love was not very high; but still, think of it—a Royal wedding. Early in the morning of Monday, the 27th November, 1837, the Royal one-horse carriage drove down to the Old Church, and there the "King of the Rooks" was married to the "Queen of the Beggars," or, to descend to plebian language, John Cole—shoemaker, otherwise known as King Cole—who lived in the Rookery, whence he took his Royal title, was married to Mrs. Simpson, who kept a beggars' lodging house known as "The Beggars' Opera," in one of the old cottages that lie back about 50 yards off the south side of the Brighton Road, just west of South Grove. The townspeople were very interested in this wedding, and were much relieved when it had taken place, as the old Queen was known to be somewhat fickle, and cast her affections about rather carelessly: once before she had betrothed herself to a tramp and had the banns properly published: on the appointed happy day, however, instead of a wedding they had a stand-up fight, and then parted, never again to meet on friendly terms.

The next Royal event was the Coronation of Queen Victoria, which took place on Thursday, the 28th June, 1838, in beautifully fine weather. Early in the morning the Church bells began to peal. All shops were closed by 11.30 a.m., when the children in the town—about 800, including myself—assembled in the Church Causeway; each child was provided with a knife, fork, and mug, and a ticket on which was printed "Victoria, Crowned 28th June, 1838." Headed by the band the procession marched round the town, and then to the Swan Field, so called from its connection with the "Swan Inn," West Street. This field, when I first knew it, reached from the backs of the houses on the north side of West Street right across to the south-west side of London Road, and from the backs of the houses and sheds on the west side of the Carfax to the east side of what is now called Springfield Road. There was but a footpath with an outhouse or two where Albion Terrace is now. In this field the townspeople assembled to make merry. There were several booths into which barrels and barrels of beer were rolled and quickly consumed by people anxious to prove by their drinking capacity their devotion to the Throne. There was also a temporary wooden bandstand erected, upon which the old Town Band played and drank, and drank and played again. Some people danced, others tried to dance, but had partnered too early in the day with "John Barleycorn," and so couldn't. A substantial dinner of roast beef and plum pudding was provided for the poor in the field, and also for the inmates of the County Gaol and the Workhouse at their respective institutions. Public dinners were also given at the "Anchor" and "Richmond" Hotels, and a ball at the "King's Head." Sports and amusements of all kinds were enjoyed till the evening, when there was another procession round the town, but by this time there was a large number of people who could not join in the second procession—they were, in fact, unable to leave the field. As, at about dusk my father and I left for home, we were obliged to take a very crooked path in order to avoid treading on the bodies of these patriotic fellow-citizens, who, representing every point of the compass, helplessly lay about, thoroughly prostrate in their loyalty—one of the most drunken days that I remember.

It was in this year I first saw a match struck. With the tedious difficulties of the old "tinder box" I was familiar enough. Many times I had heard the flick, flick, flick accompanying mother's patient and often protracted efforts to get a light from it, and my youthful mind had anticipated no better means of ignition. When, therefore, a school chum, the son of a commercial traveller, said to me "Harry, my father has got some matches, and if you only rub them like this"—drawing his hand down his sleeve—"they will catch fire," I promptly called his statement a terminological inexactitude (spelt in three letters), but he took me to his house and astonished me by proving his word.

Another event that was celebrated on a large scale at Horsham was the coming-of-age, on Saturday, the 7th October, 1843, of C. G. Eversfield, Esq., of Denne Park. The whole parish was then one scene of rejoicing; a large white flag was fixed at the top of the Church steeple early in the morning, which was ushered in by a merry peal on the Old Church bells. The day was beautifully fine and not cold. At 12 o'clock the band paraded the town, and then marched to the Vicarage, where 750 children were waiting; all joined in singing the "Old Hundredth," accompanied by the band, and then marched to Denne Park. Every person in the parish had an invitation to be present, and over 3000 people accepted it. All sorts of sports and amusements were provided, one of which was that of racing by boys after Dutch cheeses down the big hill. On Monday evening there was a grand display of fireworks on the Gaol Green, including a large set piece on a frame, "CHARLES GILBERT EVERSFIELD," and a dinner to tradesmen at the "Richmond Arms Hotel," presided over by Mr. William S. Stedman, solicitor. Young Mr. Eversfield was absent from these festivities, though at home on Monday and Tuesday, the 8th and 9th January, 1844, when two fancy-dress balls were given, one in a large room temporarily built close to the mansion, the other at the "Richmond Arms Hotel." Jullien's celebrated Orchestra, from London, provided the music at both, which were attended by large numbers of the nobility and gentry, who came in their pair-horse and four-horse carriages from all round the neighbourhood.

A very similar celebration took place in 1822, my father told me, upon the coming-of-age of Robert Aldridge, Esq., of St. Leonard's Forest. Everybody who chose to go was most generously entertained. These festivities lasted a week, beginning on Monday, the 1st July. The Church bells were rung every day. Tuesday was the great day, when 7,000 people were present. A huge baron of beef, 35 stone, was roasted in the open air. Between 700 and 800 sat down to dine at two tables, one 150 feet long, and another, horseshoe-shaped, 320 feet long, both under canvas. One interesting feature of the dinner was the presence of four old people sitting together, whose combined ages totalled 375 years: Widow Edwards, 100; Reuben Baker, 95; John Lamper, 90; John Hunter, 90. Dr. Rickword, of the Carfax, presided and the "Sussex Band of Musick" played the "Roast Beef of Old England" and other tunes. Amusements of all kinds—donkey racing, walking the bowsprit, climbing the greasy pole—were provided, as were also many hogsheads of ale, and at 10 o'clock at night 'twas impossible to walk in any direction without stumbling over the inanimate devotees of "John Barleycorn"; the most prevalent idea of the scene was said to be that of the dead and dying on the field of Waterloo.

Speaking of Waterloo reminds me there were several Waterloo veterans in the town and neighbourhood when I was a boy. Every year on the anniversary of the great battle, June 18th, these old soldiers—about 20 or 30 of them, including Old King Cole, Cobbler Will, and Jim Shoubridge, who had fought in every one of Wellington's battles—used to meet and march round the town. Some of them had left a leg in Belgium, and manfully stumped along with their wooden substitute. Afterwards all were treated to a good substantial dinner at one or other of the public houses, sometimes "The Oak," at Warnham, by Mr. Broadwood, of Lyne. These old chaps used to find a lot to talk about and settle, and usually finished up late at night at the "Lamb," where they drank a lot more liquor than they had shed blood at the battle of Waterloo.

DAN ROBERTS, THE LAST TOWN CRIER, IN LIVERY,
Born 1757, Died 1831.

I remember my father speaking of Horsham's last flash Town Crier and Beadle, old Dan Roberts, whose portrait I give. He died about 1825. From my father's description he was the most gorgeous person the town ever possessed—famous not only for his magnificent appearance in blue cloth coat with red collar and large gilt buttons, broad brimmed pot hat with gold band, plush breeches, yellow silk stockings and low shoes with silver buckles, but for his *big nose*. This worthy, like most people at Horsham in the old days, had a great regard for the Public Houses, and frequently enjoyed a drink at the "Anchor" with the Duke of Norfolk—who, as Lord of Horsham, was his master—when he visited the town. He was one day, I have been told, standing in Middle Street, contemplating the "Punch Bowl," his favourite house, from the other side of the street, allowing his imagination to run inside among the bottles of spirits and barrels of beer. So lost was he in these pleasant rambles that he did not notice the approach of a team of horses and a waggon, till the carter shouted "Hi, master, will you turn your head so that I can get my team down the street?" "Oh, certainly," replied old Dan. He then seized his nose with both hands and turned it down the street, alongside the shop windows, so that the team could pass. My eldest sister, when she was cross, used to draw sketches on paper of old Dan and his nose, an exercise that relieved her feelings and invariably brought the whole household to smiles. At the "Punch Bowl" the customers once arranged a Nose Club Meeting and Competition; Dan was awarded first prize, and my father, who enjoyed the possession of a pretty good "beak," came next—he was, however, given but fifth prize; there was no second, third, or fourth.

The first Town Crier I remember was Mills, a shoemaker; after him came old Dolly Wood, born in 1800, also a shoemaker. He possessed an excellent and clear carrying voice; I have, when walking round the Mill Bay, oftentimes heard him crying in West Street, and could distinguish some of the words he spoke. In the forties, when the price of flour had fallen 1½d. per gallon, the Horsham Millers laid their heads together and agreed to reduce the price but ½d. per gallon. Some of the wags engaged Dolly to cry round the town for three consecutive days: "Oyez! Oyez!! On account of the cheapness of corn, the liberal millers of Horsham have kindly consented to reduce the price of flour ½d. per gallon." This little job must have afforded him considerable satisfaction, as he was not only well paid, but could also enjoy the reflection that when his father kept the Town Mills, he earned the reputation of the "honest miller." After Dolly Wood's death Mills was again the name of the crier. He also had an excellent voice, which he retained to the last, dying but a few years ago, upwards of 90 years of age, the oldest crier in the kingdom.

Closely allied to the Town Crier, by the nature of their appointment, were the Night Watchmen. The last two in Horsham were Jack Sayers and Isaac Aldridge. To these two worthies the custody of and responsibility for the town during the night were committed. Many times I have heard them cry out in their nocturnal peregrinations, "'Tis past 12 o'clock, and a stormy night," or similar remarks according to the facts upon the time and weather. There was another kind of Night-watching that used to be regularly undertaken at Horsham—as indeed, elsewhere, generally—about 1819-22, and that was watching for "Resurrection Men," or body-snatchers: men who used to prowl round Churchyards, after dark, to dig up freshly-buried bodies and, at a price, carry them to London to be sold for dissection. People who could afford it used to pay two or three men 2s. 6d. or 5s. each per night to watch for a fortnight the grave of their departed relative, to see the body was not stolen; many times the old cottages on the edge of the Churchyard, and the Belfry itself, have been used for this purpose.

Jack Sayers, better known as " Jack Chaff," was a chaff-cutter by trade, and used to nearly always carry his chaff-box and cutter about with him on his back. He was a comical, happy kind of customer, always singing or whistling, yet frequently getting into hot water over something or other. One Sunday he went to Church service the worse for liquor. The beadle, in his uniform, told him to go out. "What," he exclaimed, "be putt out by a livery sarvant; no that I wunt." But put out he was though; in fact, he was too drunk to offer much resistance. On another occasion he was up before the magistrates, to whom he was well known, for a debt of some kind (this was before the days of County Courts). " Why don't you pay ? " he was asked. " Well, gentlemen, the fact is I'm stiver-cramped." " Stiver-cramped ! what does that mean?" " It means, gentlemen, that I'm satchel-sprung." "Well, what does that mean?" " What, don't you gentlemen know what that means ? It means I'm augur-plugged." The magistrates laughed, and let him off as lightly as they could.

" Good old Isaac," as Aldridge was called, besides following his trade—that of carpenter—held other offices in the town. Up to about 1840, when the Fire Brigade was organised, with tradesmen in pot hats as firemen, Old Ike was Horsham's only fireman, and had sole charge of the small squirting apparatus that we boys admiringly called an engine. This was kept in an old shed where Manor Place is now, and I think must have been the identical engine presented to the town in 1780 by Lady Irwin, of Hill's Place, "an engine capable of throwing 120 gallons of water a minute." This formidable instrument used to take Old Ike about three-quarters of an hour to put together and get into working order when its services were required at a fire. He was also organ-blower and bell-ringer at the Old Church till he died. He further undertook the repairs of the Church steeple, putting new shingles where wanted. But important as these offices seemed to us, it was as big drummer to the old Band that Ike used to afford us the greatest satisfaction. When there was a band job on he would be sure to have sought inspiration in an extra glass or two, and then he would delight us boys by his extraordinary drumstick flourishes, and his industrious accompaniments to the Band's favourite melodies — " Hearts of Oak," " Bonnie Dundee," " Bonnets of Blue," " Rory O' More," "The Brighton Camp," &c. These tunes, with perhaps a few others, used to constitute the Band's repertoire. Music in band parts being in manuscript only was hard to get and very expensive. It appeared, too, to be the subject of much misunderstanding among the bandsmen, and some of the harmonies were certainly rather hard for the public to appreciate, especially towards evening at the Broadbridge Heath and other club feasts where the Band was engaged to play. I give here a list of performers with instruments in the old Band, about 1835 :—

Edward Potter, sen., Trafalgar Road ...	Flute and Fife.
Edward Potter, jun., Trafalgar Road ...	Clarionet (leader).
Abraham Lintott, Normandy ...	Clarionet.
George Lintott, West Street ...	Clarionet.
Edward Peters (" Darby "), The Common	Key Bugle.
William Potter, Trafalgar Road ...	Key Bugle.
James Potter, Trafalgar Road ...	Trumpet.
Joseph Potter, Trafalgar Road ...	Trombone.
Harry Potter, Trafalgar Road ...	Trombone.
Old Wyndham, Queen Street ...	French Horn.
Peter Potter, Trafalgar Road ...	Serpent.
Isaac Aldridge, London Road ...	Drum.

There was yet another official in the town familiar enough in my boyhood's days, but whose occupation will seem a queer one to the present generation. I refer to the "Beggar-pooker." At that time there were lots of sturdy beggars about, hardened to their career, experts at poaching and promiscuous foraging. They were better fed and happier than many hard-working country labourers. Sometimes they would have a donkey to carry their kit, cooking utensils, &c., and often a tent with which they would encamp on one or other of the many strips of roadside waste land, which as yet had not been thoughtfully taken by the landlord of the adjoining property. In the towns as well as the country these beggars were frequently a great nuisance. They would, perhaps, get a foot in the doorway of a private house, and by threats obtain from timid people money or food. There were as yet no police who could be sent for, but it was one of the duties of the Parish Constables to move beggars away, a duty they dare not refuse if they were offered the fee of 1s. This duty they delegated to the Beggar-pooker. The last two, both of whom I can remember, were Ned Potter and Tim Scott. Old Ned was a capable officer, whose assistance out of the parish the beggars didn't much relish; but Scott had the character of a malingerer. I have seen them many times ridding the town of troublesome rascals. For this purpose they were armed with a pole about 6ft. long and nearly as thick as the wrist, and if the gentry to be helped out of the town did not move at the desired pace when requested, they would find the pole tickling their ribs or the smalls of their backs. Old Potter was one day pooking a beggar away up the North Parade, when Squire Tredcroft happened to be walking down towards his residence, Manor House. "What are you pooking there, Potter?" he asked. "Man been begging, Sir," was the reply.

"What do you want to beg for, my man?" he then asked the beggar. "I've had my kettle stolen, Sir, and I want to buy another." "How much is a kettle?" "Eighteen pence, Sir." The squire gave 1s. to the beggar, who, instead of thanking him for it, cheeked him for another 6d. "Pook him off, Potter," said the old gentleman, "pook him off, pook him off." Beggar pooking was not always an easy job. My eldest brother was one day at Guildford, when he was accosted by a beggar. "You come from Horsham, don't you?" "Yes," he replied. "Is old Potter, the Beggar-pooker, still alive?" "No," replied my brother, "he's dead." "Oh, is he," said the beggar, "then I can go to Horsham again; the last time I was there that old — poked me all the way down the Bishopric out of the town, but when we got to the bottom I up with my fist and knocked him head over heels. I bolted off then, and have never been there since."

The first professional policeman at Horsham was Gower, whom we boys regarded—at first—with fear, appointed October, 1839. Afterwards, with him, was Tuppin; then came Green, the first superintendent; he was cross-eyed and broken-winded, and was promptly nicknamed "Old Blowfly."

Another public servant, though not an officially-appointed one, was Ned Hall, the waterman. At a time when each household depended for water upon its own well, and that, perhaps, not a deep one, the supply was rather precarious. Well water at Horsham, too, was very hard, and most people used to save all the rain water they could for washing purposes, &c. With his pony cart and barrel old Hall could always in summer time do a good trade in water, which he used to fetch from the river, selling it at a half-penny per bucketful, and with a wooden trough, fitted behind the barrel, watering the streets, charging 1d. per time for watering the road in front of a house. This money the old man used to collect once a week; at the houses of those who did not pay he used to cut the water off, making the streets into an interesting patchwork of wet and dry.

The most thoroughly disliked man in Horsham was one Charles Feist, better known as "Greenacre," a native of the town. He was a shoemaker by trade, but in this sedentary occupation of leather working he was unable to satisfy his ambitions, and so, getting attached to a lawyer's office, very soon picked up enough knowledge of law to make it useful to himself and extremely unpleasant to others. He thus became known as "Lawyer Feist." A big fat man, with a red face and whiskers: with his appearance, hard heart, loud voice, determined manner and unscrupulous character, he was, in different ways, an object of terror alike to the poor and well to do. He fulfilled the unpleasant office of bum bailiff with a callousness and dishonesty hardly credible. His duty once took him to the house—or rather hovel—of a poor labourer at Two-Mile-Ash, who had got into debt, and whose wife was lying ill abed with a new baby. Armed with his legal process, and untouched by the pitiable circumstances, he literally took the bed from under the poor mother and child. Such inhuman conduct is sure to breed a desire for vengeance, and shortly afterwards the friends of this poor woman had their chance of taking it. Meeting old " Greenacre " at a fête up in the old cricket ground, in North Parade, they surrounded him, and breaking off the legs of some of the seats, belaboured him right and left to such an extent that he was laid up for some time; yet though this castigation softened his skin it did not soften his heart, for in 1837 he paid one of his professional visits to a Mrs. Jenkins, the wife of a labourer at Wild Goose. This unlucky pair had placed themselves in the power of the machinery of the law, and as one of its merciless cog-wheels "Greenacre" went to grind out of them the creditors' dues. His character had preceded him, his visit was anticipated, and its result was tragic indeed. Burdened by debt, by the perpetual struggle for the bare necessities of life—as indeed most labourers were burdened at this time—and by a large family, which she was shortly expecting to increase, the unfortunate woman, in her rage and despair, met the hardened limb of the law with an axe, and threatened to cleave his skull if he did not retire; but this threat she lacked either courage or opportunity to carry out, for instead she fell dead at her tormenter's feet. This incident gave him his execrable nickname "Greenacre" —a fiend of that name having but just been capitally punished in London. This nickname stuck to him for the rest of his life; fortunately he left no descendants to inherit either it or his bad qualities.

Quite a different specimen was poor Billy Claytor, the simpleton referred to on page 42. He was Horsham's odd handy man : with his lisping tongue, perpetual smile, soft tread, civil and obliging ways, he had the manners, without the hypocrisy, of Uriah Heep, and always seemed to be, without using words, unnecessarily apologising for his existence. He maintained himself, in bachelor simplicity, on the few shillings he earned till middle life, when he inherited about £450. This little windfall developed his manly virtues, which were quickly appreciated by a stranger, a young London lady, willing to share his joys—and his cash. Immediately after marriage they set about dissipating both, and as soon as the latter was exhausted, the lady left him to do his best with his sorrows and empty pockets alone. He returned to boot and window cleaning in a chastened and philo-

sophic mind. The following lines, by an esteemed
Horshamite, were written upon Billy's return :—

WILLIAM CLAYTOR: HANDYMAN OF HORSHAM.

Poor Claytor is come back again,
    And well enough he might,
Four hundred pounds and more 'tis plain
    He's fooled away outright.

Poor fellow, he begins to see
    The sad effects of folly,
Reduced again to poverty
    He feels quite melancholy.

With plenty he was not content,
    He needs must cut a swell,
And by that means his money went,
    And that he knows full well.

Not only that, he took a loft
    At Herring's, near the square;
He furnished it with carpets soft,
    And trinkets rich and rare.

He bought two watches and a clock,
    And glittering chain and seals,
A silver-mounted music box
    To cheer him at his meals;

A fine pianoforte quite new,
    Of mahogany 'twas made,
Elegant chairs and tables, too,
    Were tastefully displayed.

A quantity of books he bought,
    Among them Shakespeare's plays;
Napoleon's life, and how he fought
    The English in old days.

The room in fitting up, 'twas said,
    Cost thirty pounds, or more;
Saucepans and pots beneath his bed,
    He had at least a score.

He bought a dozen pairs of shoes,
    Clothes more than he had need;
'Twas his delight to read the news
    And smoke his favourite weed.

His room complete, he must invite
    His neighbours in to tea,
And new-made friends came every night
    His little room to see.

He always kept a little gin,
    A little port and sherry,
When any of his friends came in
    He liked to made them merry.

But music Claytor could not play,
    Though music he had plenty;
His education I should say
    In music had been scanty.

He could the barrel organ play,
    And sure you can't deny it,
You'd laugh to hear him grind away
    That grand old tune, " Be quiet !"

For want of elbow grease and oil,
    For want of proper care,
His furniture began to spoil
    Though none the worse for wear.

But Claytor's was a bachelor's life,
    And that he could not bear,
He longed to take himself a wife
    His happy lot to share.

Says he ! this chance I'll not let slip,
    To change my single life,
To Brighton town I'll take a trip
    To seek me out a wife.

And there he went a month or two,
    And then came back again,
He said that Brighton was no go,
    He could no wife obtain.

Said he, there was beyond dispute
    A lot of ladies there,
But as I thought that none would suit,
    I thought I'd try elsewhere.

To visit London now he turned,
    To seek a wife—the elf;
Soon with a lady he returned,
    More foolish than himself.

He soon made her his wife, and she
    Like him must cut a dash,
And thus between them both, you see,
    Away went all their cash.

His furniture he now must sell,
    His books and music too;
To watches, chains, and seals as well,
    He now must bid adieu.

All sold, to London town again
  They both go off together;
While she his money could obtain,
  Her love was tough as leather.

A year passed by, then back again
  Poor Claytor comes once more,
To everyone it is quite plain,
  As bad off as before.

He's left his pretty wife behind,
  His money is all spent,
He's only now to call to mind
  How foolishly it went.

His money gone, his wife away,
  He's in a pretty plight,
Few in this town I think will say,
  But that it serves him right.

Another harmless character was poor Harry Lambert. Most Horsham people of old and middle age still carry in their minds impressions of his extraordinary appearance, but few can remember when he was born. I can see him now an infant in the lap of luxury, dressed in fine silks and satins, being wheeled about in a perambulator by his nurse. As he grew up it became evident Dame Nature had been somewhat remiss in her favours to him, and had left him in a rude and unfinished state physically and mentally. As a mature individual his low brow, thick black hair and ragged whiskers, squint eyes, hollow cheeks, lantern jaws—from which proceeded a voice that would silence a factory hooter—and his carbuncle close to his nose, rivalling it in size and beating it a colour, all combined to make a face that would turn bankrupt even the beautifying powers of the late Madame Rachel. But his attractions were not all upon or in his head. Had a giant pair of hands taken him by the head and heels and pulled him out straight he would have been tall, but he appeared rather undersized. He was hump-backed, with his chin where his chest ought to have been, and knock-kneed; each foot grew a crop of corns and a bunion,

E

and these, with his rigid ankles and knee joints, both fixed at an angle of about 60 or 70 degrees, and a kind of bobbing forwards and backwards at the waist imparted a very peculiar gait as, dressed in his suit of black with frock coat and pot hat, he went his way about the Town. A first chapter of Genesis scientist, a Book of Revelations philosopher, and a staunch thirty-nine article theologian, Harry culti- vated sufficient confidence in himself to give his views on these subjects to the clergy, afterwards, as he used to say, "hearing them spoke from the pulpit word for word." He had his humorous side, too, and was always composing conundrums. "When the sun shines on the north side of the old Church steeple, what will be the length of a piece of string?" Such was the kind of problem with which, to his delight, he would puzzle some of his friends, whilst with original astronomical observations he would astonish and enlighten others. Poor Harry, he had need of some such pleasures, for he was the butt of everyone's practical joke, and was induced to go on many "owl- catching" and other expeditions that turned out most uncomfortable for him. On one of these occasions Harry was stripped naked and painted green all over; another time he was pegged down on the ground with croquet hooks and treated with various indignities. His love adventures, too, were numerous and enter- taining; many well-to-do ladies have been at one time and another the object of his sincere affection, but they were all, alas, also sources of great disappointment. Intensely desirous of success in his last amorous affair, Harry sought the aid of two friends—a fatal request;—these were trusted to convey his letters to the new object of his love, and always brought him back the most satisfactory answers. By means of these letters a meeting of Harry and his new love was arranged for one dark night under the Normandy

RACE BETWEEN HARRY LAMBERT, ALLEN ALDRIDGE, AND FOOT'EM JENKINS,
On Good Friday, about 1879.

wall, whence an elopement was also planned. Harry was there at the appointed time and his susceptible heart was soon put into a flutter by the appearance, just over the wall, of a bonnet—*the* bonnet. Bidden to approach his lady, he obeyed, only to get the Arun Steam Mill flue cleaner in his face and a bucket of water all over him.

Two lesser lights among Horsham extraordinary characters were Allen Aldridge, the Old Church organ blower, who in many respects resembled Harry Lambert, and "Foot'em" Jenkins, window cleaner, truck shover, &c., remarkable for his short legs— upon which his ready-made trousers appeared like extended concertinas — and his long splay feet. Everyone of these three individuals was interesting in himself; when they combined to entertain the public the fare provided was rich indeed. This they once did on Good Friday afternoon, about 1879, when they ran a race, arranged by a few sportive in- dividuals, from the "Hurst Arms" Inn to Thornton's Beer Shop (now known as "The Stout House"), on the Carfax, for a gallon of stout. I give a carica- ture, by a well-known Horsham Artist, of this famous event.

Another Horsham couple who used to entertain us boys at the fairs and clubs around were old Joe Waight and his young wife—Joe was twenty-five years older than she;—they made quite a respectable pair, and were very affectionate to each other. Dressed up and assisted by his wife, Joe used to excite our admiration by his wonderful tricks: his most astonishing feat was that of submitting to be shot at by his wife. "Now, Joseph," she used to say, "I am going to shoot you!" "What for, my dear?" Joe would ask, alarmed; her only reply was a bang, as she pulled the trigger of a big pistol. Joe jumped as if shot, and then, unhurt, he would hold up between his finger and thumb the very bullet she had shot (so we supposed) which, marvellous to relate, he had caught in his hand just as it was about to enter the region of his heart ! ! !

Quite a notorious character was old Whiting, the sweep, and quite as notorious a place was the beershop he kept, a dilapidated old house on the south side of East Street, just about where the " Bridge House " now stands, which was known as the " Beggars Lodging House." Here many beggars, who had been pleading disease and poverty in the daytime, would enjoy a beefsteak and onion supper, and spend a rollicking evening together. Besides beggars, tramps, and later, German bands, old Whiting had thousands of other inmates, with whom, or rather with which, the place was tremblingly alive. The more respectable inhabitants used instinctively to pass by on the other side of the road ; but to some of the youths of the town the place was attractive enough, for there they could drink and gamble, and play "bumble-puppy" and "devil among the tailors" until very late at night, and all day on Sunday. It was, in fact, the resort of bad characters in the town ; night rows were frequent, sometimes serious, occasioning many visits to the Town Hall by old Whiting, whence he always returned lighter in pocket after being interviewed by the magistrates and settling up with their legal adviser and clerk, Mr. Dewdney Stedman. Notwithstanding heavy fines, and the fact that he could neither read nor write, the old man with his equally illiterate but very careful wife, his disreputable beershop, and chimney sweeping, managed to save several thousand pounds.

Two of the most notorious characters I ever knew were Charley Price, known as old "Patch Price," and Charlotte Venn, known as "Cherry Ripe." Price was an ugly little brass-whisker'd man with a club foot ;

dressed in a pot hat, red neckerchief, white smock
frock, drab breeches, and white stockings; on his
good foot he wore a low shoe with a flash buckle; on
his other foot he had a thick boot. Venn was the
mother of Hewett, the murderer of Smith, and no one
who knew her could wonder at her breeding a criminal
son. She wore a black coal-scuttle bonnet, a fancy-
coloured shawl, short dress, and white stockings. This
precious couple used to attend the fairs, markets, club
feasts, &c., in Horsham and the neighbouring villages,
each with a basket, Price selling pies and cakes,
and Venn selling sweetbread, whelks, fruit, &c., &c.
Price was always quarrelsome, and drunk as often
as he could get enough liquor to make him so;
frequently the pair would get drunk together, and
then the public ear would be assailed by the most
awful specimens of mutual execration. Charley
had a well-to-do sister, who lived in a nice little
house in Brighton Road, and when he had drunk
all his money he used to replenish by serenading
her with such shocking language that she used to
throw him money out of the bedroom window to get
rid of him. At election times his voluble and abusive
tongue, well moistened, would produce words hot
enough to make Satan jump; he always appeared
on nomination and polling days, when, mounted
on someone's back, through being so short, he
would hurl his very choicest at whichever candidate
had been unfortunate enough not to secure his
services.

Charley Price was the last man put, as an offender,
in the Horsham Stocks, a punishment he had many
times before sustained, always for the same sin—
drunkenness—and the last time he ever got sober in
this way was about 1834. The Stocks used to stand
on the Gaol Green, somewhere near where the Bandstand is now; soon after Price's last occupation of

them they were burnt in a spree on the 5th November. New ones were made, but never contained the legs of an offender; they were kept at the south end of the Town Hall, and were used but once when Bunk Dumbrell and Walter Burstow got into them for the purpose of being photographed by Mr. T. Honywood, the captain of the Horsham Fire Brigade, who introduced the new art into Horsham. They were many years afterwards fixed in their present position at the west end of Richmond Terrace. Punishment by Pillories and Stocks was legally abolished in 1837. But though offenders ceased to be put in the Stocks, the treatment they afterwards received was not much better; they were confined in what used to be called the black hole, a dark dungeon place under the Town Hall, reached by steps leading down from the street. I've seen many a prisoner given a shove down into the miserable place, where he had to remain, visible to the public through iron bars, till bailed out or tried. Males were confined on the West side and females on the East side of the building. Compassionately disposed people would sometimes give the unhappy prisoners tobacco or cakes or what not through the iron bars. Children, too, would sometimes give them trifles in much the same way as they would give to animals at a menagerie. This treatment of prisoners continued till the new Police Station was built in 1846, just east of where the County Gaol in East Street had stood.

Another instrument of cruelty on the Carfax—the Bull ring—was practically neglected longer ago than is popularly supposed. It is true the last bull was baited as late as 1813. Many people appear to think that this " sport " was frequently and regularly indulged till that year, but it was not so. Mr. Gilburd, my old master, who was born in 1804, told me he well remembered that in 1813 the bull ring was quite covered over with dirt and grass, and had to be "found" for this last occasion, and that he could remember no previous indulgence of the pastime. This evidence would seem to prove that several years elapsed between the last and the next last occasion, and we may further infer that the "sport" had already fallen into disrepute when Mr. Warner, the hatter (afterwards known as "Bull" Warner), and others, in the exercise of their humane feelings, set up an agitation against it, and organised sufficient sentiment in the town to put a stop to it here for ever. Quite as widely spread, if not so widely believed, is the legend that the bulls liked being baited, and if not fetched in good time would break loose and go up to the Carfax "on their own." The last bull did not appear to be at all well-disposed, and upon his appearance young Gilburd, with all the alacrity of youth, hopped over the fence that then lined the west side of the Carfax, and climbed a tree, whence he watched the last exhibition of this kind of barbarity at Horsham.

Another public exhibition of barbarity, also the last of its kind at Horsham, took place on the 6th April, 1844, when John Lawrence was hanged for the murder of Mr. Solomon, superintendent of Police at Brighton. From time immemorial all executions for the County of Sussex had been carried out at Horsham in public, and always attracted large crowds of people. There had been no execution here since 1836, when Sheppard and Sparshott, two young men, were hanged together. Lawrence's execution was fixed for Saturday, 6th April, at 12 o'clock noon, the day of Horsham Teg Fair this year; April 5th, the usual fair day, being Good Friday. East Street, from Park Street right up past

the Gaol, was thronged with people, estimated at
about 3,000, including myself, all waiting to see the
sight; many of them had walked in long distances
and from all quarters. Among them was Lawrence's
brother; I did not see him, but was told he was
drunk and boasting that he was a greater scoundrel
than the condemned man, though he had never committed murder. Mr. Kenrick, the curate, did a very
sensible thing in prevailing upon the schoolmasters
in the town to march the scholars up Denne Park, out
of the way, so that they should not witness the scene;
but a great many children, and women too, were
present. Costermongers from Brighton and elsewhere were selling gingerbreads and oranges. " If
any man says I'm idle, let him wheel this truck
of oranges up from Brighton. These are beautiful
oranges. They'll melt in your mouth like butter,
run down your throat like a wheelbarrow; they are
sugar outside, brandy in the middle, and the rind
will make you good boot soles." Old Whiting, at
his beer-shop, was doing a roaring trade, and expressing a wish that a man were hanged every day.
Pedlars were walking to and fro, singing and selling
printed copies of the following " Last Dying Con-
fession " :—

> Good people all I pray draw near,
> A dreadful story you shall hear :
> Overcome with grief and fear,
>   I am condemned to die.
> I do lament, and sore repent,
> The evil deed which I have done ;
> My time is come, my glass is run,
> I now behold my setting sun—
>   All in the prime of life.
>
> Chorus—
> John Lawrence is my name,
> To grief and shame,
> I brought myself this world may see,
> Young men a warning take by me,
> At Horsham, on a fatal tree,
> Alas ! I am doomed to die.

I was brought up at Tunbridge Wells,
Where once in honesty I dwelt;
But now, alas, how sad to tell,
   For murder I must die.
As you may read, a dreadful deed
I did commit in Brighton Town,
Where I went pilfering, rambling down;
But hark! I hear that dreadful sound—
   Lawrence! prepare to die!   Chorus.

As through the Brighton streets I rolled,
A piece of carpet there I stole;
The justice on me did seize hold,
   Oh! fatal was that day.
You understand, poor Solomon
I with a deadly poker slew,
And took away his life 'tis true;
And there, exposed all to my view—
   My victim I beheld.   Chorus.

'Twas thus I murdered in his prime,
A father dear and husband kind,
And caused him for to leave behind—
   How awful to unfold;
Borne down with grief to sigh and weep,
Eleven orphan children dear,
Besides a tender wife we hear,
For which my end is drawing near—
   Oh Lord, look down on me!   Chorus.

To Lewes I was sent at last,
Tried, and the dreadful sentence passed;
I was guilty found, and quickly cast,
   To die upon a tree.
I do bewail, in a gloomy gaol,
My fatal end is drawing nigh,
To thee, Oh Lord, I pray on high,
To grant me fortitude to die,
   Upon the fatal tree.   Chorus.

Adieu, my aged mother dear,
Don't gieve for me, dry up those tears,
For I must stay no longer here,
   I'm numbered with the dead.
The fatal tree now bends to me,
While English justice loudly cry,
Blood for blood, prepare to die,
I see grim death before my eye,
   Awaiting for his prey.   Chorus.

Good people all in each degree,
I pray that you'll be warned by me,
And shun all evil company
    Before it is too late.
I assure you all, 'twas my downfall,
From honesty, alas, to stray,
And to bad company I gave way,
On me have mercy, Lord, I pray,
    And all my sins forgive.   Chorus.

The Mother.—To her Condemned Son.

It was in Brighton, as you may see,
There was committed a tragedy,
By one John Lawrence, all in his prime,
He did commit the dreadful crime.

As Mr. Solomon was standing by,
He with the poker did him destroy,
He took his tender life away,
Then asked for a knife himself to slay.

[*Mother.*]

Farewell, my son, my only son,
Thy short life course is almost run,
And fast the hour approaches nigh
When you, my darling son, must die.

Although thou, alas, art much to blame,
And brought thyself and me to shame;
Although the world thy name despise,
Thou still art precious in my eyes.

Though all mankind thy foe shall be,
Yet I will fondly cling to thee;
A love a mother's heart can feel,
Not words, but actions, can reveal.

I nursed thee in thy infancy,
And watched thy useful tendency,
And fondly hoped to see that day
When you my kindness could repay.

But ah! a sad reverse has proved,
The child whom I so fondly loved,
Is doomed to die a death of scorn—
I wish my son had ne'er been born.

The tears shall never leave my cheek,
Some lonesome residence I'll seek,
And with my aged locks of snow
Will to the grave in mourning go.

The gallows—a ghastly-looking affair of timber and

SUSSEX COUNTY GAOL, HORSHAM.   ERECTED 1775, PULLED DOWN 1845.

canvas, both painted black—was erected on the west front of the County Gaol, which stood just east of where the Railway Bridge in East Street is now, on the north side of the road, with the front facing Denne Park. A large body of London Police patrolled up and down in front of the Gaol. At 12 o'clock the prisoner, pinioned and in a very penitent frame of mind, appeared and mounted the scaffold. A white cap was put over his head, and the rope round his neck; then, whilst the chaplain was reading the Burial Service, the bolt was drawn, and the last malefactor executed at Horsham went to his doom. The body was buried "within the precincts of the gaol," just about behind where the Jireh Chapel in Park Terrace East now stands. When the gaol was pulled down, in 1845, the body was exhumed and temporarily taken to the "Queen's Head" stables, where it excited the curiosity of a good many people, who paid 2d. to see it. Subsequently it was buried in the west end of the old Churchyard, where the bodies of scores of victims of the scaffold at Horsham had preceded it.

I give a reproduction of a painting by myself of the front of the Sussex County Gaol at Horsham, just before it was pulled down in 1845. The cross **X** shews the spot where Lawrence was executed.

Horsham began its agitation for railway service in 1834. The first line proposed and surveyed for was named the "Grand Southern Railway," better known, perhaps, as "Stephenson's Railway," and was to have been made from London through Dorking, Horsham, and Shoreham, to Brighton. Much excitement was caused in the town by the prospect, and the large house now known as Sussex House, formerly called the Pioneer, opposite the Tanyard footpath, which was built as the prospective "Railway" Hotel, still stands a monument to the speculative enterprise called forth. But though the town supported the scheme by public meetings and favourable evidence at the Government Enquiry, it fell through, chiefly, I have been told, because the price asked for the necessary land was so much higher than that of the alternative Three Bridges scheme, which was adopted. Nothing further was heard again of Horsham railway accommodation till 1838, when meetings were held to support the proposal of a branch railway from Horley. That also fell through, and not till 1844 did there again appear any further prospect, when three different schemes were brought out, viz.: a direct London to Portsmouth line through Horsham; a continuation of the "Epsom Atmospheric Railway" through Dorking to Horsham; and a branch line to Three Bridges. The Portsmouth line seemed to promise most benefit to the town, but the branch line seemed most likely of realization, and as the townspeople had waited now so long and got somewhat impatient, a petition signed by over 500 of them in favour of this was presented to Parliament. A Bill embodying its principles was presented to the House of Commons on the 6th June, 1845, and, without opposition, became law on the following 5th July. On Monday morning, the 19th Feb., 1848, the new line was opened for traffic. The station terminus here was but a little plain wooden structure standing about midway between the present Station and the "Railway Hotel." A great many people went up to see the departure of the first train. There was no ceremonious send-off, but there was a public dinner at the "King's Head" in the afternoon, at which Mr. Henry Padwick presided. I was present when the first train steamed out of the station. It was not a very long one, but as the first journey was free of expense it was very full. Some of the cars were covered and some were open; these latter—the 3rd class—were at once nick-named "rubbish carts." When steam was put on the wheels of the engine would not bite the rails, and the train would not move, but the application of a little sand made matters right, and amid cheers the first trainload of people started its interesting journey.

Three events every year were always looked forward to and well kept up when I was a boy, and for many years afterwards. They were May Day, July Fair, and 5th November Bonfire Day. May Day, or Garland Day, was a very jolly time for us youngsters, not only because it was a holiday, but also because we used to pick up what seemed to us quite a lot of money. Early in the morning we would get up our best nosegays and garlands—some mounted on poles —and visit the private residents and tradespeople. We represented a well-recognised institution, and invariably got well received and patronised. People all seemed pleased to see us, and we were all pleased to see one another, especially if the day was fine, as it now seems to me it always was. At Manor House special arrangements were made for our reception, and quite a delightful old-time ceremony took place. Boys and girls gaily decked out for the occasion, a few at a time used to approach the front door, where a temporary railed platform was erected, and there old Mrs. Tredcroft—a nice-looking, good-hearted old lady—used to stand and deal out to each and every one of us kind words and a few pence, everyone curtseying upon approach and upon leaving. Old Mrs. Smallwood, who lived in a quaint old cottage in the Bishopric, always used to go round on May Day with an immense garland drawn on a trolley by two or three boys. On the top of her garland she used to mount her little model cow, indicative of her trade—milk selling. Gaily dressed up herself in bows and ribbons, she used to take her garland round the town, call upon all the principal residents and tradespeople, to whom she was well known, and get well patronised. This old lady lived nearly 100 years, and until she was nearly 96 regularly carried milk round to her customers in buckets suspended from a yoke on her shoulders.

On this day, too, we had Jacks-in-the-Green. The chimney sweeps used to dress up in fancy costumes and in evergreens and flowers, and, accompanied by a fiddler or two, parade and dance all round the town and neighbourhood. There were two sets of Jacks-in-the-Green when I was a boy—the Potter and the Whiting parties—and considerable rivalry existed between them. Lady Shelley used to patronise them handsomely by giving them plenty to eat and drink, and a good round sum of money. She one year gave the Whiting party a new set of dresses, fitting them out in a very gay manner. The children, with their flowers and garlands, finished their part of the day's proceedings about noon, but the Merry-Andrew parties kept the game going all day, getting merrier and merrier as time went on, till the evening when, the fiddlers still scraping away, and now producing sounds so queer that it was comforting to reflect they had no smell to them, they would all retire to old Whiting's beershop and finish up.

The youth of to-day can have no idea of what the Horsham July Pleasure Fair was like seventy years ago, nor of its importance as a means of providing fun and entertainment. Entertainments and shows for the working classes were very scarce; now and again a circus would come round, and there were the few Friendly Societies' feasts. The Broadbridge Heath Club feast was perhaps the best of its kind; nearly all the Rookery people and a great many other Horsham people used regularly to patronize it. The members, most of them in white round frocks, some in their fluffy old beaver pot hats, some carrying a new willow stick partly peeled, and every one decorated with a coloured ribbon bow, used to march in to a service at the Old Church, then back again to Broadbridge Heath to their feast and amusements: but none compared in attractiveness to the July fair. The business part of the fair was confined to one day only, but the pleasure fair lasted any number of days from three to nine. It began always on the 18th July, and if that fell on Saturday, Sunday, Monday, Tuesday, Wednesday or Thursday, the fair finished on the following Saturday; but if it fell on Friday it began on that day and continued till the following Saturday week. On these days the country people flocked into the town by hundreds and thousands. The Carfax, from North Street right down to the Town Hall, from London Road to South Street, and from East Street to West Street, the whole available space was covered with all sorts of booths, shows, cheapjacks, roundabouts (chiefly worked with a winch by hand), and shooting galleries; boxing and acrobatic performances; fat women and living skeleton shows; drinking booths, pickled salmon tents, whelk and fruit stalls, all doing brisk business with crowds of people the day long. The proprietors of these shows and stalls, their families and assistants, used to live in their caravans and tents in the Carfax during the fair; their crude sanitary arrangements being a source of much annoyance and sometimes of disease to the permanent residents there. The drinking booths used to have a bush out over the entrance to indicate the nature of the trade done within; several houses, too, on July and November fair days used to put out boughs, and were known as " bough houses," or temporary drinking shops. As a boy I used to go out in the country for people and get bushes and small boughs of trees to be used for this purpose.

The house now No. 30, Carfax, "The Carfax Café," was always a bough house at these fairs. The fair also attracted a large number of pick-pockets, roughs, and cheats of all sorts, many of whom were on their way to Lewes or Brighton Races; gentry, whose contributions to the proceedings, usually tendered at the drinking booths, would sometimes turn the place into a pandemonium: special constables used to be sworn but did not always suffice to cope with the business. In 1835 there seemed to be an extra number of roughs about: on Saturday night, between eleven and twelve o'clock, in consequence of a disturbance the constables attempted to clear one of the drinking booths, kept by a man named Rhodes. One of the roughs asked Mr. Clarke, a headborough, by what authority he ordered them to quit the booth; Clark shewed his staff, which was immediately taken as the signal for a fight. About fifty of the roughs collected, and, arming themselves with the legs of chairs and forms, which they smashed up, attacked the constables and soon got the upper hand; they then sallied forth round the town in a body, knocking down and robbing anyone who got in their way, until at length a sufficient number of townspeople collected to withstand them. A general riot and fight then took place during which, I have been told, the Riot Act was read from the Town Hall steps. Fifteen of the roughs were apprehended and put in the black hole that night; five were taken at Roffey and two at Warnham the next morning, and all were sentenced to various terms of imprisonment. The duration of the pleasure fair on the Carfax was reduced to one day only in 1874, by an order from the Home Secretary; and by another order in 1886 it was removed from the Carfax altogether. Its shadow still annually appears in the Jews' Meadow. I give a sketch of it in full swing about 40 years ago.

HORSHAM JULY FAIR.

Although the July business Fair was a sheep fair, and the November Fair a colt fair, occasionally animals of quite a different kind were sold at them. I have been told of a woman named Smart who, about 1820, was sold at Horsham by her husband for 3s. 6d. She was bought by a man named Steere, and lived with him at Billingshurst. She had two children by each of these husbands. Steere afterwards discovered that Smart had parted with her because she had qualities that he could endure no longer, and Steere, discovering the same qualities himself, sold her to a man named Greenfield, who endured, or never discovered or differently valued, the said qualities till he died.

Again, at the November Fair, 1825, a journeyman blacksmith, whose name I never heard, with the greatest effrontery exhibited for sale his wife with a halter round her neck. She was a good looking woman, with three children, and was actually sold for £2 5s., the purchaser agreeing to take one of the children. This "deal" gave offence to some who were present, and they reported the case to a magistrate, but the contracting parties, presumably satisfied, quickly disappeared, and I never heard any more about them.

The last case happened about 1844, when Ann Holland, known as "pin-toe Nanny," or "Nanny pin-toe," was sold for £1 10s. Nanny was led into the market-place with a halter round her neck; many people hissed and boo'd, but the majority took the matter good humouredly. She was "knocked down" to a man named Johnson, at Shipley, who sold his watch to buy her for the above sum. This bargain was celebrated on the spot by the consumption of a lot of beer by "Nanny," her new husband, and friends. She lived with Johnson for one year, during which she had one child, then ran away—finally

F

marrying a man named Jim Smith, with whom she lived apparently happy for many years.

The celebration of the Gunpowder Plot has varied in degree considerably in my time, and in my father's time, but it has always been carried out in some form or other till now, when less attention is being paid to it than at any other time I can remember. Its periods of decline and revival have taken place according to the coolness or enthusiasm of the inhabitants, or the opposition or indifference of the magistrates. It is clear, from a Proclamation issued by the Bailiffs in 1779, that there was a conflict of opinion between the local authorities and some of the inhabitants, as to the advisability or manner of holding a celebration that year.   The Proclamation reads :—

NOTICE.

" Whereas a scandalous and infamous paper hath been stuck " up against the Market House (*i.e.*, Town Hall) of this Borough, " by some wicked and ill-designed person or persons, in the " words and figures following, viz. :—

G " Man, if you will believe us advising you for your " own good, all you that have least hand in trying to
F " prevent the fire and fireworks in the Town will come " best off, for it is determined betwixt us to have a fire " of some sort, so if you will not agree to let us have " it in peace and quietness, with wood and faggots, we " must certainly make a fire of some of your houses, " for we don't think it a bit more sin to set your " houses afire, and burn you in your beds, than it is to " drink when one is thirsty. We don't do this to make " a talk and a chavash about Town only, but so sure " it is wrote on paper, so sure by God Almighty we " are in earnest.   For we should desire no better " diversion than to stand at a distance and see your " houses all in flames.   Gentlemen, we shall take no " money nor anything else to go out of the Square, for " that is the place we have fixed upon."

" Now we do hereby offer a reward of 20 guineas to any person " or persons who shall inform against the offender or offenders " who actually wrote and stuck up the said bill, to be paid on " the conviction of such offender or offenders by us.

" Nov. 13th, 1779."   " WM. ELLIS, ⎱ Bailiffs.
                                    " WM. JONES, ⎰

It would seem that a very interesting celebration was contemplated by some people in 1779; whether it actually took place or not I do not know. Four years later, however, several people were indicted for assisting in making a fire on Nov. 5th, but from about this time right up to 1845, when the magistrates again interfered, Horsham never went without a regularly arranged bonfire on Nov. 5th. Sometimes there were three separate bonfires and parties, one, the largest, on the Carfax, another (ours) in the Bishopric, and the third down in the Collyer's School Croft. There were no factory-made fireworks about seventy years ago; most people who took an active interest in the proceedings made their own, and very strong ones they were. I used to make lots of them for my mother to sell, as well as those I made for my own use. I remember an amusing adventure with one of these home-made fireworks—a big " serpent." There used to be on the " Crown " side of the " Lamb " a very small lock-up shoemaker's shop, used by old " Cobbler Will," the old soldier referred to on page 46; he was a queer-looking little man, with a large head, and fists like legs of mutton; as he used to stand at his door, with his apron on, his appearance was so goblin-like as to frighten some of the passengers who came in the coaches that then used to pull up at the " Crown Inn." On one November 5th he was at work in his little shop when Bob Reading opened his door, put in the live serpent, then shut the door and held it so that old Will could not get out. There were some lively moments whilst he and the serpent chased each other round the little room, which quickly filled with smoke, and from which old Will was presently allowed to emerge, vowing vengeance, and declaring that he had not had a hotter time at the battle of Waterloo. Several parties used to parade the town during the day, each with a guy seated

in a chair, those in charge singing the old doggrel,
" Remember, remember, the 5th November," .&c.
In 1870 " The Horsham Bonfire Boys " Society was
formed, and by it the affair was organised into a
splendid celebration, in which nearly the whole of
the population seemed to join.   Scores of people were
disguised and dressed up in all kinds of fancy
costumes; huge guys, 10 and 12 feet high, were
made and paraded round the town in a long procession, with bands, trees of fire, and various performers in vans, on horseback, and on foot.   On the
Carfax a bonfire was made so large in later years
that it scorched the paint on some of the surround-
ing houses.   The Horsham celebration in the early
seventies was one of the best in the Kingdom.

St. Crispin Day, the 25th Oct., used also to be well
celebrated at Horsham, but it was regarded as an
affair of the shoemakers, whose patron Saint Crispin
was, and every one of them could on that day be depended upon to get thoroughly drunk in his honour.
The townspeople generally were interested in the day
because it was made the occasion for holding up to
ridicule or execration anyone who had misconducted
himself or herself or had become particularly notorious during the year.   An effigy of each offending
person—frequently there were two together—was on
Crispin Day hung on the signpost of one or other of
the Public Houses, usually in the district where he or
she resided, until the 5th November, when it was
taken down and burned.   For several weeks before
the day people would be asking " Who is to be the
Crispin ? "   The first " Crispin " I ever saw was hanging outside the "Black Jug" in North Street, when I
was quite a tiny little shaver ; I never knew whom it
represented, nor what the offender had done to get
himself disliked.   Another year the effigies of a man
and his wife named Fawn, who lived in the Bishopric,

were hanged up on the signpost at the " Green Dragon." Together they had cruelly illused a boy, son of the man and stepson of the woman; they had also whipped him with sting-nettles. There they hung, each with a bunch of sting-nettles in the hand until November 5th, when a hostile crowd collected, some of whom went down to Fawn's house, assaulted him and smashed his hand-cart. For this they were summoned and fined £2 each, an amount quickly covered by public subscriptions. Another year old Skiver Tilley, the bootmaker, offended his brother stitchers. I never knew what he had done, but they suspended his effigy to old Whiting's signpost, up at the beggar's lodging house, on Crispin Day. Skiver came to Horsham from London, and being a particularly active and knowing member of the bootmaker's party, he was paid special honour; every evening from Crispin Day till the 5th Nov., the gentlemen of the wax went up to the beerhouse, they took the effigy in and sat it down in the tap-room, then in its company all got drunk together. The last " Crispin " was old Tolhurst, a master boot-maker. He found one of his men scamping his work, so determined they should show him the boots they were making before the soles were put on; when he passed their work he gave them each a ticket. This system might be thought commendable by some people, but with his men it was very unpopular, and so his effigy was hanged at the "Green Dragon" and labelled " Old Dollars (sic) and his tickets."

Old Tolhurst afterwards married a lady with some money, whereupon he opened a Pawnbroker's Shop at what is now No. 18, West Street—the only pawn-shop Horsham ever had—advertising that he was pre-pared to advance on goods sums of from 2d. to £500. He put out the sign, three gold balls, two at top and one at bottom, representing it was said a two to one bet that the articles pledged would never be redeemed. This was a pretty safe bet here, for the pledgers found that from the pawnbroker's inexperience, and rather generous disposition, they were able to get such high advances on their goods as to make the business, in fact, a satisfactory sale, whilst Old Tolhurst found himself in such unhappy financial circumstances that he thought it advisable to change his place of residence by the distance of two or three counties, without saying good-bye to his friends.

Yet one more day in the year to which an old custom attached was "Gooding Day," the 26th Dec. The larger gentry in the neighbourhood used to systematically distribute gifts at Christmas time. Sir Timothy Shelley, of Field Place, used to give beef away in large quantities; Mr. R. Aldridge, of St. Leonard's, used to give about 6lbs. beef and a plum pudding to about sixty or seventy families; Mrs. Fox, of Chestnut Lodge, used to give ¼lb. tea and 2s. 6d. in cash to about eighty poor old women, and 2ozs. tea and 1s. cash to about two hundred more; others gave away articles of clothing, caps, stockings, &c. Gooding Day was the recognised time for other poor people, who had not benefitted by the above distributions, to make their demands upon the charitable disposition of the remaining well-to-do people.

BELLS AND BELLRINGING.

Soon after I was apprenticed, old John Vaughan, my master's father, the Sexton and head bellringer, came into the little room where we were at work and said to me, " Henry, I think you had better come and join the ringers, we've got a few jobs coming on and we shall want some new hands." I was very pleased indeed with the prospect thus unexpectedly opened to me, and agreed at once to learn the art of bellringing, and to devote my best attention to it. There was a little preliminary business to negotiate, viz., the payment of an entrance fee of 3s., which at this time was an utter impossibility to me. An alternative was offered of ringing for the first six months without receiving any payment for it; but as within this time one or two weddings would take place, at which the ringers would be engaged and paid for their services, an acceptance of this proposition did not strike me as being very business like; however, Old John Vaughan came to my rescue by paying the fee, I agreeing to repay him from the first money I received. This matter thus settled, it was not long before I was up in the Belfry exercising my new hobby, handling the ropes with ardour and enthusiasm. When I offered to repay the old man from the first lump sum I ever received (7s.) he refused to take the money, generously telling me I might keep it. As I was badly in want of a new hat I straightway went up to Angus' shop, at the south-east corner of Middle Street, where Messrs. Tanner & Chart now are, and of my own initiative bought myself one, an act that greatly enhanced my self-importance and much pleased my dear old mother.

Perhaps a little information respecting the Old Church Bells and the old Bell Foundry at Horsham will be appropriate here, and of interest to the reader. The following extracts respecting the Foundry and the repairs to the Church Bells were taken by Mr. R. Garraway-Rice, J.P., and published in Vol. 31 of the Sussex Archæological publications.

From several parish registers it has been ascertained that at the end of the Sixteenth and beginning of the Seventeenth Centuries there was a bell foundry at Horsham, and that a considerable trade was carried on. In the Lindfield Parish churchwardens' accounts for 1594 are the following entries :—

> Laid out for expenses at Horsam for ourselves and the weneman (waggoner) his s'vnt and his cattel ... ... xiij^s iv^d
> P'^{d} to one to carrye the moneye to Horsham to the bell founder ... ... xij^d

In the Slinfold churchwardens' accounts for 1593 are the following entries :—

> Item for takyng down the belles ... ... xvij^d
> Item for hangying vp the belles ... ... xvi^d
> Item the carridg of O'r bells to horsham ... iij^s iiij^d
> Item or charges ij days at horsham about the belles ... ... iiij^s

In the same accounts for 1611 :—

> For castyng the grete Bell—
> Imprimis for carrying the bell into Horsham ij^s i^d
> It. the Castyng of the seyd Bell ... ... xlij^s viij^d
> It. for carrying the Bell from Horsham ... ij^s ij^d
> It. stocking the Bell ... ... ij^s
> It. for makyng of the bond that the Belfounder was bound to ... ... vj^d

Again in 1618 there are similar entries.

In Mr. Tyssen's "Church Bells of Sussex" it is stated that one, Richard Eldridge, had a bell foundry in Sussex from about 1592 to 1623; and in the Horsham churchwardens' accounts there are many entries that shew this same Richard Eldridge (and later his partner and successor, Bryan Eldridge, who about 1623 moved his foundry to Chertsey) was a tenant under the Horsham Churchwardens of a house and premises called the " Belle House," situate in the Normandy, at a rental of 10s. per annum. Here bells of all sizes were cast and repaired for various parishes near and far. There are still, according to Mr. Tyssen, 90 bells in the County of Sussex made by the Eldridge's. Most of those made by Richard Eldridge between 1592 and 1623 are inscribed, " Our hope is in the Lord, R E," and the date.

In the Horsham accounts are many other interesting entries showing expenditure upon the bells. Thus in 1611 :—

> Item. Richard Eldridge owed to the ould war-
> dens p^t of his rent for there yeare ...   ...   iij^s iiij^d
> Item. Received of him for his rent this yeare the
> Casting of a pare of Brasses for the great Bell   xj^s viij^d
> So the sayd Richard oweth the pish in mony
> and for 1℔ of Brasse mettell   ...   ...   xx^d

On August 19th, 1615, during a severe storm, the steeple was struck and set afire by lightning, and a poor girl, Elizabeth Stroode, who was standing by the belfry door, was killed. The lightning did a great deal of damage, necessitating the re-casting of the big bell, new shingling of the steeple, and many other repairs, according to the following entries in 1616 :—

> Imprimis layd out to William Dean and Helpers
> to new trusse the great bell   ...   ...   xij^d
> Item payd to William Dean for mending the
> Steeple   ...   .   iiij^{ll}
> Item payd to the Shingler for shingling the
> steeple   ...   .   x^{ll}
> It. spent on them that put out the fires of the
> steeple   ...   .   xiiij^d
> It. spent upon the Shingler when they came to
> take the work   ...   .   viij^d

Item spent upon helpers to pull up and downe
the bell ... ...   viij^d

Item Layd out for Ironwork about the bell,
Steeple, chimes and the howse in the Normandy ... ...   xvij^s

It. spent upon the bell Fownder in coming to
take the bell ... ...   vj^d

Bellfounding just about this time appears to have
been in a prosperous state at Horsham, for the Bellhouse, or Foundry, was enlarged or re-built, and was
afterwards known as the New Bellhouse.

Amongst the payments for the same year (1616)
are the following :—

Imprimus payd to Richard Eldridge the mony
remayning due to him for casting of the
great bell ... ...   xj^{ll} x^s

Item payd him for casting of a brass for the
4th bell ... ...   iij^s

Item payd to George Lullingstone for timber
and mending of the Bellframe and for new
stocking of three of the bells and other work
about the Bells ... .   iij^{ll} xvj^s ix^d

Item payd for fetching of weights and for
drawing of the Bell to the pitt and from
the pitt ... ...   iiij^s

Item pay'd to Stephen Russell for Iron Coales
and workmanship and mending the gret bell
Clapper ... ...   v^s vi^d

Item pay'd to Thomas Tanner for timber and
work to make a Jyne to weigh the Bell ...   iiij^s iiij^d

Item payd payd to Roger Wood for making a
band (*i.e.*, bond) for the Bell ... ...   vj^d

Item for 1 hundredweight of mettell to put in
the great bell ... ...   iiij^{ll}

Item payd for careing ij^l of mettell ... ...   vj^s viij^d

Item payd in earnist to George Marlen to stock
and hang the great bell ... ...   xij^d

Item payd to William Dean for 2 dayes work
with the bell hanger ... ...   iij^s

> Item pay'd to Philip Ginden and Thomas Morgins for puting out of the fier in the Steeple ... ... x^s
>
> Item payd to Robert Honiwood for an Iron hooke to weigh the great bell ... .. xij^d

In 1619 the Horsham Bell Foundry again underwent alterations and repairs, as will be seen from the following :—

> Item payd for timber and stone for the new bell house ... ... xxx^s
>
> Item payd for Lime and Mull (Marl) ... iij^s vj^d
>
> Item payd to Thomas Clarke for nailes and a dogge of Iron for the same howse ... ... iij^s vj^d
>
> Item payd for 3 ridge tilles ... ... iiij^d
>
> Item payd to William Deane for his work about the new bell house ... ... x^s
>
> Item payd to Henry Salter for his work about the new bell house ... . x^s
>
> Item payd to Richard Mitchell for his work about the Church and the new bell howse ... x^s

There appears to have been a running account between Richard Eldridge and his successor on the one hand and the Horsham Churchwardens on the other for many years; sometimes the Churchwardens owed a balance for re-casting or repairing bells, and then it would seem that the bells being in order and requiring no attention, Eldridge would get behind with his rent. Thus in 1619 appears :—

> Arreareges Richard Eldridge for the new bell Howse ... ... x^s

Again in 1620 :—

> Item received of Richard Eldridge for 2 yeares rent of the new bell howse ... ... xix^s

Then on the other side :—

> Item payd to Richard Eldridge for casting of 3 payer of Brasses and for more mettell to put to them ... ... xxix^s 8^d

Item payd to William Deane and his man for 2 dayes work taking out of the bell brasses and laying of them in againe   ...   ...   v^s

Item payd to William Streate Carpenter for his journie and his Charges to take the worke about the bells   ...   .   v^s vi^d

Item payd to Hamlet Borer for carreing of a load of Timber to mend the bells ...   ...   iiij^s vi^d

Item payd to William Streate Carpenter in pte of payment for his work about the bells   ...   x^s

Item paid him more for his work in pte   ...   xxx^s

In 1621 :—

Item received of Richard Eldridge for one years rent of the new Bellhouse eanded at the Anounciation last past   ...   .   x^s

In the same year, on the other side :—

Item payd to Richard Eldridge in p^t of payment for the casting of the fourth bell accordinge to his bargain as appeereth by a noate   iiij^{li}

Item layd out to William Streate for comming and taking downe the 4th bell and for hanging of hir vp againe and to John Mulford for his help and his Tackling   ...   .   xv^s iiij^d

Item payd for sending one for William Streate   xij^d

Item layd out and spent vpon Helpers to take down the bell, and drawing of the bell to the Pitt and from the pitt, and for pulling of the bell up againe   ...   .   xij^s vi^d

Item payd for 18 new hoops for the new bell wheels   ...   .   xviij^d

In 1622 appears the last entry respecting Richard Eldridge's tenancy of the Bellhouse, his rent being apparently then again in arrear :—

Richard Eldridge, for the new bell howse, his rent ...   .   x^s

In the same year, on the other side :—

Item payd to Richard Eldridge toward the casting of the Fowth bell   ...   .   x^{li} x^s

Item payd to John Mulford and helpers, and for his tackling and new waying of the 4th bell ...   .   xj^s

Item payd for sending of the Beame to Warnham Fornaise   ...   .   iiij^d

It is an important and interesting fact that the period up to which bells cast by Richard Eldridge are found is 1623, being the same year that he disappears from Horsham, and it seems highly probable that it was at that time—or two or three years before—that Bryan Eldridge, the successor of Richard, established or took the Chertsey Foundry.

In 1633 the Horsham Churchwardens decided to make the big bell much heavier, for in the accounts that year appear :—

Imp^{rs} paid to Bryan Eldridge, the Bellfounder, for casting the great Bell, and for mettell added to her, for wee agreed with the said Bellfounder at 12^s ye hundred for casting, and 5^l 12^s a hundred for the mettall added to her. The said great bell before she was cast weighing five and twentie hundreds and a quarter, and now weighing twentie seven hundredes and three qte^{rs} as neere as could be ghessed ...   .   xxiiij^{ll} j^s

Itm paid to William Lintott for carrying the bell to and from Chertsey and his charges there   ...   .   iij^l xv^s iiij^d

To ye Bellhangers for taking downe the Bell: hanging her vp and theire other worke about the rest of the Bells, for their coming, horse hire to bring their Pullies and tooles and their helpers at divers times about the loading, weighing, and hanging the said bell ...   iij^{ll}

Our charges for o^r selves and o^r horses at Chertsey to see the bell cast and weighed, being 4 of us and 3 daies out   ...   ...   i^{ll} ix^s vj^d

For a bond from the Bellfounder to the Churchwardens for ye warrant of the bell ...   ...   j^s

For a piece of Timber to make a Beame to weigh the bell, for making and carrying the same, for other timber and paile and raile to mend the Churchyard fences ... ... x^s

To Richard Clerke for his worke and yron for the beame to weigh the bell, as about all the bells, theire clappers and other furnitures, as also about the clock and chimes ... ... j^l vj^s viii^d

In 1645 the big Bell, which seems to have had more attention given to it than all the others together, was again sent to Chertsey to be again made heavier, and the following entries appear :—

Received for 8 pound of bell mettle hewed from the bell ... ... viij^s

Of the Batchellors of the pish toward the casting the bell ... ... j^l xviij^s vij^d

Paid to John Burstow for the gin to weigh the bell and for bringing him to the church ... vij^s vj^d

Paid to Evans Prise for fetching and careing the ffornace Beame and waites severall times j^s xj^d

Paid the helpers when the bell was taken downe ij^s vj^d

Paid to Mr. Thomas Sheppard for making the bonds for the security for the bell ... ... xviij^d

Paid for helping loade the bell ... .. ij^s

Paid for James Mulford for taking downe the bell and hanging vp ... ... xxx^s

Paid to John Rowland fore careing the bell to Chertsey and back againe ... ... iij^l x^s

Paid for o^r expenses for our horse meate Goinge to Chertsey, and to the bellfounders helpers there ... ...j^l xvij^s vj^d

Paid to the bellfounder for his work and for 3 hundred and 3 quarters of Mettle put into her more, the bell waing 32 hundred xxxiij^l viij^s

Paid to William Wheeler for mending the greate bell clapper ... . x^s

In 1652 the 3rd bell was taken down and recast:—

Imprimis paid to Bryan Eldridge for casting ye 3rd Bell ... ... x^{ll}

It. paid to him for Mettle to put in the bell ... 1^{li} 15^s 0^d

It. for o^r Journey to Chertsey and o^r expences 1^l 2^s 4^d

It. paid for Smith's worke about the belles ... ij^l ij^s 4^d

It. paid to William Brigs for taking doune the belle and hanging vp ... ... j^{li} xv^s

It. paid for the hier of 2 horses for o^r journey to Chertsey ... ... 9^s

It. for expences vppon the Bellfounder and the helpers in hanging vp the Bell ... ... vj^s $iiij^d$

It. to Robert Tylor for careing the bell to Chertsey ... ... ij^s $iiij^d$

It. paid for work about the Chimes and Belles j^{li} $iiij^s$ vj^d

In 1717 and 1718 the bells again gave trouble, and were repaired at a cost of over £60. In 1748 and 1751 the great bell gave further trouble, and at a Vestry Meeting, held June 6th, 1751, it was agreed: " That the Great Bell should be immediately taken " down and sent to London to be new Cast by Thomas " Lester Bellfounder in White Chapple." Up to this time there were six bells only, these I was told by old Michael Turner, of Warnham (born 1796), were the heaviest set in Sussex, the tenor weighing 36cwt.; but on March 8th, 1752, at a Vestry Meeting the momentous resolve was made: " That the remaining " 5 Bells should be taken down and sent away with " all convenient speed to Thomas Lester at his " Foundry in White Chapple, London, in order (with " the Tenor which has been sent some time agoe) to " be cast into 8 bells according to articles which are " to be entered into, By the Churchwardens with the " said Thomas Lester."

On New Year's Eve, Dec. 31st, 1814, the ringers had been down early in the evening to ring the bells, and had adjourned to the "Anchor," as usual on New Year's Eve, for supper; whilst there a fearful storm raged over the town, and on their return journey to the Church, after 11 o'clock, to ring the old year out and the new one in, they found the lightning had

struck down two of the large elm trees that then
lined the Causeway, and when they got back to the
belfry they further found that the steeple had been
also struck by lightning, that the seats fixed to the
belfry wall had been torn away and scattered about
the room, and that the second and seventh bells were
cracked. The cost of repairing these two bells, by
Thomas Mears, of Whitechapel, was £65 13s. 8d.
The last disasters in the belfry happened in 1838.
John Vaughan and his sons Jim and Joe were pulling up the big bell for a funeral when, somehow or
other, the clapper went the wrong way. Old John
told Joe to go up and turn her; just about as Joe
got up to the bells the others heard a tremendous
bang, then all was silent. Old John and Jim were
much frightened, thinking Joe must have got hurt,
perhaps killed: they shouted up the stairs, but got
no reply; tremblingly they went up to the bells, and
there, to their intense relief, sat Joe in silent contem-
plation. "Why, what's the matter," they asked;
"That's what I want to know," replied Joe. An
examination shewed that whilst Joe was unhurt, the
bell was cracked right down one side, and therefore
rendered quite useless. The re-casting of this bell
by Thomas Mears cost £45 15s.; taking down and
re-fixing, by Jas. Ridge, £12; and the carriage to
and from London, by Jas. Lloyd, the carrier, £5 7s.
A further accident on November 15th, the same year,
resulted in no damage to the bells, but considerable
damage to the Sexton. Poor old John was seeing to
his duties—oiling the bearings of the bells, &c.—when
he pitched headlong amongst them; he was laid up a
long time, with two broken ribs and a broken collar-
bone. From this time the bells worked satisfactorily
for over 50 years. In 1890 the whole of them were
re-tuned and re-hung, and the belfry ceiled at a
cost of £140, raised by public subscription. The

weights of the bells, tuned in E flat major, and their inscriptions, are now as follows :—

1— 6cwt. 3qrs. 10lbs.—Thomas Lester and T. Pack made us all 1752
2— 7 ,, 0 ,, 2 ,, —Mears, of London, fecit 1815
3— 7 ,, 0 ,, 8 ,, —T. Lester fecit
4— 9 ,, 0 ,, 25 ,, —Thomas Lester and Thomas Pack, of London, fecit 1752
5—11 ,, 1 ,, 9 ,, —Thomas Lester, of London, made me
6—14 ,, 1 ,, 20 ,, —Thomas Lester and Thomas Pack fecit 1752
7—16 ,, 1 ,, 12 ,, —Thomas Mears, of London, fecit 1815
8—23 ,, 1 ,, 7 ,, —Thomas Mears, founder, London, 1838

Rev. H. W. SIMPSON, Vicar.

JOHN THORPE,
RICHARD WALDER, } Churchwardens.
PETER WILSON,

Up to 1789 the bells were always rung from the floor of the Church, but in that year a belfry was made (at the ringers' expense of £20) about 8ft. above ground, a position much more convenient alike for ringers and churchgoers. It was fitted up with every convenience and necessary comfort. In 1864, at the restoration of the Church, the belfry was raised again and taken to its present position, level with the clock. It is a matter of pride to me that in regard to this further removal the then vicar, Rev. J. F. Hodgson, most courteously consulted the interests of the ringers in every respect. Apropos of the restoration of the Church, begun April, 1864, and finished November, 1865, the following lines "composed" on the occasion may interest the reader :—

About two years ago our Parson declared—
The Church is in danger and must be repaired:
A committee was formed and the money got in,
With pence from the poor, which I think was a sin.
London builders were asked to send tenders down,
Not a man was invited of our ancient town ;
One was selected—a great city swell,—
And how he sold townsmen I'll very soon tell.
The time flew away, near a twelvemonth went round,
Since this clever builder to Horsham came down ;
He was courted by tradesmen, the great and the small,

And to keep in their graces he dealt with them all :
This one for paint, for glass, and for lead,
That one for meat and another for bread ;
The grocer, the draper, the trader in gin,
And the dealer in game, cunning Jack, were let in.
The snob and the tailor for boots and for clothes,
The Parsons for cash, the amount no one knows.
The man at the bank when too late, alas, found,
He had given too much credit by eleven-hundred pound.
Those who supplied him with timber and rope,
Alike all were duped : for their cash they've no hope.
Other victims in Horsham this builder had many,
For now he's a bankrupt, and won't pay a penny.

It was in 1667 that the possibility of ringing 5040 changes was recognised, but a method of producing these changes was not invented till 1715, when a poor lad—John Holt—solved what had been a difficulty to campanologists. In 1766, some 14 years after they had the requisite number of bells, the Horsham ringers achieved the glory of their first 5040 changes. As this was 99 years after the discovery of its possibility, it must, I suppose, be admitted as evidence in favour of those smart people who so frequently assert that Horsham is 100 years behind the time. This belated achievement was thought highly of at the time, and a board upon which particulars of the event with the names of the ringers was then painted, still adorns the belfry wall. Any reproach that may have attached to these Horsham ringers on account of their dilatoriness was completely wiped out by their subsequent successes, for between 1766 and 1798 they got ahead of all the ringers in the Kingdom on two occasions, and established no less than nine records, particulars of which I give.

The Horsham Ringing Society was affiliated to the National Society of Ringers called the Cumberland Youths. On Friday, April 11th, 1766, rung at Horsham 5040 Grandsire Triples, the first 5040 changes ever rung in that steeple. Performed in

3 hours and 8 minutes, by Horsham Ringers, as follows :—

Harry Weller	... ...	treble
Thomas Lintott	... ...	2
William Tyler	... ...	3
John Foreman	... ...	4
Anthony Lintott	... ...	5
John Morth...	... ...	6
Thomas Bristow	... ...	7
Thomas Aldridge	... ...	tenor

The bobs were called by Thomas Bristow.

On Tuesday, May 2nd, 1775, rung at Bolney, in Sussex, by the Horsham Society, a true and complete peal of 5040 changes of Union Triples, the first peal ever rung in the County of Sussex in that method. Performed in 3 hours and 6 minutes, as follows :—

Thomas Jones	... ...	treble
William Tylor	... ...	2
Benjamin Hall	... ...	3
Edward Aldridge	... ...	4
Harry Weller	... ...	5
Thomas Lintott	... ...	6
Thomas Bristow	... ...	7
Thomas Aldridge	... ...	tenor

The bobs were called by Thomas Bristow.

On Sunday, May 26th, 1776, rung at Horsham, by the Society of Cumberland Youths, a true and complete peal of 5152 changes Bob Major, the first ever rung by this method in this steeple. Performed in 3 hours and 17 minutes, as follows :—

William Tylor, Horsham ...	...	treble
Thomas Lintott, „ ...	...	2
James Wilson, Cuckfield ...	...	3
Samuel Beeching, Bolney ...	...	4
Samuel Wood, London	...	5
Francis Wood, „	...	6
George Grose, „	...	7
Samuel Muggeridge, „	...	tenor

The bobs were called by George Grose.

On Sunday, Nov. 16th, 1777, rung backwards, at Horsham, by the Society of Cumberland Youths (all of whom were inhabitants of Horsham), a true and complete peal of 5040 changes of John Holts' Grandsire Triples, being the first peal ever rung reversed in this method by any men in the Kingdom. Performed in 3 hours 15 minutes, as follows :—

Thomas Jones	... ...	treble
Thomas Lintott	... ...	2
Benjamin Hall	... ...	3
Edward Aldridge	...	4
Harry Weller	... ...	5
John Foreman	... ...	6
Thomas Bristow	... ...	7
Thomas Aldridge	... ...	tenor

The bobs were called by Thomas Lintott.

On Monday, Feb. 15th, 1779, rung at Horsham, in honour of Admiral Keppel, by members of the Society of Cumberland Youths (all of whom were inhabitants of Horsham), a true and complete peal of 5040 Union Triples, being the first peal ever rung in this Steeple by this method, in 3 hours 12 minutes, as follows :—

Harry Weller	... ...	treble
Thomas Jones	... ...	2
Benjamin Hall	... ...	3
Edward Aldridge	...	4
Thomas Lintott	... ...	5
John Foreman	... ...	6
Thomas Bristow	...	7
Thomas Aldridge	...	tenor

The bobs were called by Thomas Lintott.

On Monday, June 13th, 1785, rung at Uckfield, by members of the Society of Cumberland Youths, a true and complete peal of 5040 Grandsire Triples, being the first peal ever rung in that Steeple. Performed in 2 hours 57 minutes, as follows :—

Thomas Jones, Horsham	...	treble
Thomas Lintott, ,,	...	2
Benjamin Hall, ,,	...	3
Edward Aldridge, ,,	...	4
Harry Weller, ,,	...	5
John Foreman, ,,	...	6
Thomas Bristow, ,,	...	7
James Wilson, Cuckfield	...	tenor

The bobs were called by Thomas Lintott.

On Monday, Sept. 12th, 1792, rung at Leatherhead, by the Horsham Society, a true and complete peal of

5040 changes of Grandsire Triples, the first peal of Grandsire Triples ever rung in that Steeple. Performed in 3 hours 1 minute, as follows :—

Thomas Jones	treble
Thomas Lintott	2
Anthony Lintott	3
Edward Aldridge	4
Harry Weller	5
John Foreman	6
Thomas Bristow	7
William Oakes	tenor

The bobs were called by Thomas Lintott.

On Sunday, Jan. 5th, 1794, rung at Horsham, by the Horsham Society, a true and complete peal of 5040 changes of Grandsire Triples, performed in 2 hours 59 minutes, the quickest performance of the kind ever known on bells of the same weight, the tenor being 24 cwt., as follows :—

Alexander Luxford	treble
Anthony Lintott	2
Thomas Lintott, sen.	3
Edward Aldridge	4
Thomas Lintott, jun.	5
Thomas Jones	6
Thomas Bristow	7
William Oakes	tenor

The bobs were called by Anthony Lintott.

On Tuesday, May 1st, 1798, rung at Horsham, by the Horsham Society, Mr. Holt's original peal of 5040 changes of Grandsire Triples. This was known as "the highest and most accurate peal ever composed." The method of calling it was invented by James Bartlett, who on this occasion rang fifth bell. Performed in 2 hours 55 minutes, as follows :—

Thomas Jones, Horsham	treble
Charles Barber, Kensington	2
James Lintott, Horsham	3
Richard Downe, ,,	4
James Bartlett, Kensington	5
William Bottomley, Halifax, Yorks	6
Anthony Lintott, Horsham	7
John Foreman, ,,	tenor

The bobs were called by James Bartlett.

There is no knowledge of a complete peal of 5040 changes having been performed since 1798 till 1810, and from 1810 again till 1818, and lastly on Wednesday, the 10th October, 1821, rung at Horsham, by the Horsham Society, a true and complete peal of 5040 Grandsire Triples, performed in 2 hours 59 minutes, as follows :—

George Jones	... ...	treble
Thomas Lintott	... ...	2
James Whybrow	... ...	3
Isaac Aldridge	... ...	4
Thomas Jones	... ...	5
William Oakes	... ...	6
Thomas Lintott, jun.	...	7
John Vaughan	... ...	tenor

The bobs were called by Thomas Jones.

After this the enthusiasm engendered by the possession of the new set of 8 bells in 1752 seems to have completely expired.

The high standard of excellence attained by the Horsham ringers of 1766-1798, attested by the above records, almost makes me wish I had been born a century before my time, so that I could have shared the honours they reaped; for, alas, when I joined in 1841 all the old skilful ringers had been dead many years. "Ichabod" was written over the Belfry door. The ringers of this time—John Vaughan, Edward Vaughan, Jas. Duffield, John Vaughan (the younger), Harry Vaughan, Ned Sturt, Joe Vaughan, Joseph Hopkins, and Ike Aldridge—and those for many years afterwards were unable to ring changes at all, and could not understand and appreciate the records made by their predecessors.

I was exceedingly enthusiastic in my new hobby, and whilst myself learning to ring, took what will seem to the reader a strange kind of pupil. I was always very fond of birds, and of other animals too. Of birds I kept a great many—tom-tits, yellowhammers, blackbirds, starlings, jackdaws, &c.—my

favourite was a starling "Jack." I had brought him up and taught him to speak, so I thought I would also teach him to ring. Accordingly, I fitted a little bell with a rope in his cage, and taught him at my sign to pull the rope with his beak, and make the bell ring, and continue pulling till I signalled him to leave off. He was an apt pupil, and we grew very fond of each other. I could always leave his cage open without fear of losing him. Several times he flew away, but came back again alright; once he was away for three days. When I saw him returning I used to call out "Come on, Jack," "Come on, Jack," and he always seemed pleased to let me catch him.

From time immemorial it had been the custom to ring bells every Sunday morning, all the year round, to let the inhabitants know the time. At 7 a.m. the third bell was pulled up and rung for five minutes, at 8 o'clock the first and second bells were chimed, and again at 9 o'clock the seventh bell was pulled up and rung for five minutes; every evening, too, from Michaelmas to Ladytide, at 8 o'clock, the Curfew was rung on the fifth bell. I was soon trusted to fulfil these little offices and used to take a delight in them that some of my elders did not understand, especially in ringing the Curfew. I used to love the weird re-echoing sound up in the steeple, in the dark, above my head. I remember enjoying myself one night in this way, when Harry Vaughan burst into the Belfry door. "Here, what the —— does this mean: I've been hearing you ringing for twenty minutes, as I walked from Picts Hill, you only ought to ring five minutes." With that he snatched the rope out of my hands, threw me out of the Belfry, and slammed and locked the door. I was able then to see what an enormity I had committed in giving the Curfew bell an extra quarter-of-an-hour.

Old John Vaughan, the sexton, was as straight and upright a character as ever lived. He would never lie, nor trim an unpleasant truth; would never do, nor knowingly profit by a mean trick. He and I had a great regard for each other. By some he was regarded as quite a paragon. Old Trush Taylor, who lived in the Normandy, was one day asked by the Vicar, Mr. Simpson, why he did not go to Church: "Because I don't want to," he replied, "I wants to be more like Mast'r Vaughan, and less like the parsons." But it must be admitted that with these and other virtues old John had a quality or two that could not be classed with them: he had an uneven temper and a despotic inclination which were neither in accordance with the sweetness of the bells, nor conducive to the study of campanology; sometimes, indeed, he would lock the Belfry up and refuse to let us ring at all. On one such occasion, just after I joined, on New Year's Eve, we had been down and rung the bells early in the evening, and had adjourned, as usual, to the "Wonder" beerhouse—later called the "Talbot," at the Town Hall end of Pump Alley—there to wait till 11.30, the usual time to start ringing the Old Year out; something or other, however, induced a fit of crabbedness in the old man, and he vowed we should not return to the Belfry that night. He was not appeased by frequent doses of alcohol—of which, indeed, all partook except myself, who was then but a boy, anxiously waiting to do my turn at pulling the New Year in—nor by the arguments of Ned Sturt who, as the best spokesmen, was very conciliatory, reminding him of the time-honoured custom now almost due to be repeated, and of the large number of people who would be disappointed by his determination if persisted in. As time crept on, arguments got to remonstrances and threats, and finally the two began tussling. They had got to the pitch of pulling each other round the tap-room, and had just broken a chair in the scuffle, when Sturt's wife appeared on the scene. She summed up the situation at a glance, and immediately brought to bear upon it the militant qualities of the modern suffragette; seizing a leg of the broken chair she flung it bang at Old Vaughan, catching him right on the chest. "You under-minded old rascal you, I'll teach you to interfere with my man—*Clear Out!*" And clear out we all did quickly; old John's obstinacy, which Ned was unable to overcome, instantly subsided, and the tussle was immediately adjourned or drawn. Ned Sturt was condemned to the effect of the vote of a woman for the rest of his life apparently, for he never came ringing any more; whilst the rest of us, in our eagerness to avoid further offending the suffragette, almost tip-toed back down the Causeway, just in time to pull the bells before the clock struck twelve. I am glad to say that during the 65 consecutive years that I helped ring the Old Year out and the New Year in at the old Horsham Church we all of us always, with this one exception, spent the evening harmoniously together.

Isaac Aldridge was about the only ringer here who possessed any intelligent idea of change ringing, but he was by no means a really good ringer, as I afterwards understood; most of the time in the belfry was spent in aimlessly ringing or chiming the old Queen's Changes—1, 3, 5, 7, 2, 4, 6, 8—&c., an occupation that by no means satisfied the ambitions I had engendered and was now nursing; for I had heard of the successes of the old Horsham ringers, as set forth above, and of the doings of other ringers round about.

My first knowledge of good ringing was got from the Warnham ringers. On Christmas Eve, 1846, I was standing with a brother ringer, Wm. Norket, at the bottom of the Bishopric; 'twas a clear, frosty evening, with the wind in the north, and as we stood we heard the six Warnham bells ringing beautifully. I proposed going over there, and we started at once. When we arrived we found old Ike Aldridge ringing treble, and the others in the following order: Frank Osborne, 2; Michael Turner, 3; John Hogsflesh, 4; Ned Turner, 5; Michael Charman, 6. They were ringing scientifically; everything seemed to be so nice and lively, and as regular as clockwork. I had now been ringing some time, and I felt ashamed of the Horsham ringers. As we walked home with Ike Aldridge I ventured to comment upon the superiority of the Warnhamites, but he was not disposed to admit it: "Pooh," he said, "they are a rough lot; they rush and tear about like tigers." After the visit to Warnham I felt I should like to go to Newdigate to see change-ranging done at its best. The Newdigate ringers at this time enjoyed the reputation of champions: Mr. James Broadwood, of Lyne, was so proud of them that he gave out, on their behalf, a challenge to any other sett of ringers in England to ring for £500; but it was not taken up. When, therefore, Ned Turner, of Warnham, offered to take me to see Tom Gadd, the Newdigate head-ringer, I felt very proud indeed. One Saturday afternoon we walked to Newdigate together, and he introduced me: "Tom," he said, "here's a lad that'll ring you a 720 first time of trying." Gadd eyed me rather doubtfully, remarking, "Well, he looks as if his head is screwed on right." We almost immediately went to the belfry, and had just pulled the bells up ready to start when a message came from the Vicarage to the effect that we must not ring, as someone was ill in the house. To be deprived of the honour I had been looking forward to just as I had got the rope in my hands was keenly disappointing to me. Observing this, Ned proposed that he, Gadd, and I should walk to Ockley, four miles away, and try a ring there, as the best to be done under the circumstances, and this we did. With three of the Ockley ringers we rang a 720 plain bob right through without a word. When we had finished old Gadd looked at me: " Do you mean to say you've never rung that peal before? " he asked. " I've never tried before," I replied. I was delighted to find I had made a good impression upon so important an individual, and it resulted in a warm open invitation to Newdigate as often as I liked to go. I went there regularly and frequently, and took to proper change-ringing as a duck takes to water. The company of the ringers, too, I found very enjoyable, and they always seemed pleased for me to come. Alec Gadd lent me their ringing book to copy out; this I did, committing the changes to memory. The next time I went up I was asked if I could sing a song. " Yes," I replied, " I'll sing you ' Boney's farewell to Paris,' if you'll let me ring the College Exercise peal with you." " What? " they asked, " can you ring that; that's a rum 'un? " " I know every wrinkle in it, and I can ring every blessed peal you've got in your book," I replied, confidently. So it was agreed. I sang the song, they were delighted; we rang the College peal, and thenceforth I was on the regular staff, so to speak, of the Newdigate ringers. Every Saturday evening I walked there—8 miles,—arriving about 7 o'clock. We rang up to 10 o'clock, and then all of us ringers and friends used to adjourn to the " Six Bells " Public House for a jollification, drinking and smoking and song singing in turn. I was just in my element; I knew so many songs at this time that I sang them a fresh lot every time I went: they knew but few, and these I quickly learnt and added to my stock. We invariably kept the merriment going up to 12 o'clock, after which I used to walk home, usually arriving between 2 and 3 o'clock in the morning. My father and mother did not much like my keeping these late hours. "Ah, my boy," Father used to say, "you'll get your nob cracked one of these nights." My intimacy with the Newdigate ringers got so warm that they tried to induce me to live amongst them, offering to build me a shoemaker's shop if I would consent to do so: one would dig the foundations, another would do the bricklaying, whilst yet another undertook to do the carpentering, &c.; but I preferred to live in my native town of old Horsham, where I had continued ringing all the time. Indeed, circumstances soon after their kind offer compelled me to cease my regular attendance at Newdigate, for I was now visiting other belfrys in the neighbourhood. My enthusiasm and skill as a ringer, and my success as a song singer, brought me invitations from places for miles around, and made me welcome wherever I went. At many of the places I visited I was asked to undertake teaching the natives the art of change-ringing, and as the task was a congenial one, and a paying one to boot, I readily undertook it.

These pleasant duties caused me a good deal of walking, as I used almost always to have to walk certainly to or from (generally both ways) the villages I attended, and this fine exercise acted as an antidote to my sedentary occupation—bootmaking. At Crawley, for instance, I was engaged one night a week for six months. The vicar, Mr. Lennard, a most amiable gentleman, was one of my pupils. He tried hard to induce me to stay there the night after ringing, perhaps up to 10.30 p.m., but I always insisted upon going home instead, and there was then no way of doing so but that of walking. At Slinfold, too, where I taught change-ringing, I was regularly engaged for some time, and greatly benefitted by the walk, my only means of getting to and fro. I sometimes on these journeys walked Nowhurst way for a change, a fact that recalls to my mind an old legend of the district.

It is said that in the time of the Roman occupation of Britain a huge bell, cast in Rome and intended for York Minster, was being carried from Chichester up Stane Street—the old Roman road that passes along the west of Slinfold—when it fell into a bog, from which the people were unable to rescue it, and it sank. It remained buried for centuries, its fate traditionally surviving down to mediæval times when witches prospered. One of these, it is said, told the people how to get the bell up again. They were to yoke a certain number of pure white heifers together, and these, by means of a long chain fixed to the bell (I don't know how the chain was to be fixed to the sunken bell; perhaps the old witch undertook to do that), would pull it up alright provided no one spoke during the operation. The old witch's instructions were being carried out, the heifers pulled well, and had almost got the bell to a place of safety, when one man, who thought the job completed, sang out, "We now have got the Nowhurst Bell, in spite of all the devils in hell." Immediately the chain broke, the bell sank back into the bog, and there it remains to this day.

My first important ringing engagement was in 1843, when Mr. C. G. Eversfield came of age. Since that time I have rung at every event at which the services of the ringers were required until 1908, when I was 82 years old, and I've missed but one or two since that—local weddings, coming-of-age of the gentry in the neighbourhood, Royal births, weddings, jubilees, and funerals (muffled bells). Occasionally we were engaged to ring without being told the nature of the event we were thus to celebrate. In 1868 we were sent down our fee, and requested to ring the bells. We did so on and off during the afternoon and evening, not knowing the occasion till afterwards, when we found we had been hired to ring in honour of the abolition of Church rates!! At my own wedding, which took place on Monday, the 30th April, 1855, another record was made in the old steeple. We had a "shoemakers' peal." Every ringer was of the same trade as I, and we rang continually all day long.

Michael Turner	...	...	treble
Ned Turner...	...	...	2
George Hobden	..	..	3
Edward Vaughan	...	...	4
Jim Vaughan	...	...	5
Harry Vaughan	...	...	6
Henry Burstow	...	...	7
Dolly Wood...	...	...	tenor

The bobs were called by myself.

This peal is still a record for Sussex, I believe.

I can honestly say that at my wedding principals and guests all kept sober; I meant it should be so, because the year before when another Horsham ringer was married I was purposely made drunk— the only time I ever was so. He had just become landlord of the old "Red Lion," which name he altered to "The Lamb," and I could see his wedding was going to be a drunken set out. All the ringers, except myself, were the worse for liquor early in the morning; some of them could hardly stagger up the Belfry stairs, and ran a great risk of hanging themselves with their bell rope. After we had rung a "mixed" peal or two the bridegroom came and gave the ringers a general invitation up to "The Lamb," but I felt sure the affair would not suit me; "No," I said, "I won't go, I don't feel up to it"; but the others insisted that I should; one of them took my watch and said I must fetch it from "The Lamb." As I, after the others, went up the Causeway, I met Mr. Richard Collins, the Parish

Clerk; such a nice old man he was, to be sure,—he was Parish Clerk for sixty years;—"Well Henry," he said to me, "whatever is the matter with you ringers, if you can't ring better than you have done this morning you'd better not ring any more." I felt his just rebuke very keenly, but had occasion later to feel still more ashamed. When I went into "The Lamb" to get my watch I was greeted with demands for a song; I sang a song, ate a little piece of cake, and drank the bride and bridegroom's health in a little brandy; then I became senseless. When I recovered I recognised my helplessness had been brought about by the determination of my companions to make my condition similar to their own, and that they had effected their purpose by means of a drug.

Quite a nice little wedding party was that of another ringer, Phil Hewell, in 1857. Everyone present enjoyed it. After the ceremony the wedding party and ringers' wives and sweethearts, about twenty-five or thirty of us, all had a merry sing-song and send-off just outside the Belfry door. An eighteen-gallon cask of good ale for the occasion had been placed under the Belfry on the night before. The day was nice and warm, and we had a most delightful time of it, drinking and smoking, chatting and singing as we sat round in chairs and on the tombstones of the old Churchyard.

On the 100th anniversary of the first 5040 changes ever rung at Horsham (see page 90), Wednesday, the 11th April, 1866, we tried to repeat the century-old performance, but I regret to say we failed, and it was not till ten years later—on Monday, Dec. 11th, 1876, my 50th birthday,—some 55 years after the last 5040 changes were rung at Horsham, that the Horsham ringers again succeeded in doing it, as follows :—

George Jenkins	...	...	treble
Elias Knight	...	...	2
William Aylward	...	...	3
Felix Knight	...	...	4
George Rapley	...	...	5
James Jeal	...	...	6
Henry Burstow	...	...	7
Joseph Hopkins	...	...	tenor

The bobs were called by myself.

Another record for Sussex in which I was concerned was rung at Warnham, on Friday, 1st March, 1889, to celebrate the installation of their new peal of eight bells, when we rung 13,440 changes, in 7 hours 45 minutes, continuous ringing from 9 a.m. to 4.45 p.m., as follows :—

George Woodman	...	...	treble
Walter Charman	...	...	2
Tom Andrews	...	...	3
Harry Cook	...	...	4
William Short	...	...	5
Felix Knight	...	...	6
Henry Burstow	...	...	7
Harry Chantler	...	...	tenor

The bobs were called by Harry Chantler.

This number of changes is just one third of the total possible to be rung on eight bells. When the Brighton ringers had their new peal of eight bells at St. Peter's, we thought they would surely beat this record, but it still holds good. The longest peal ever rung on the Horsham bells was rung on my 65th birthday, Friday, 11th December, 1891, when 6720 changes of Bob Major were rung in 4 hours 6 minutes :—

Thomas Hogsflesh	...	...	treble
Thomas Andrews	...	...	2
Walter Wadey	...	...	3
Fred. W. Rice	...	...	4
Walter Charman	...	...	5
William Short	...	...	6
Henry Burstow	...	...	7
Harry H. Chantler	...	...	tenor

The bobs were called by Harry Chantler.

The greatest number of changes I have ever rung in one week is 19,300. I once wrote out a peal of 5040 changes of Grandsire Triples. It may interest the reader to know it took a piece of paper 85 feet long. The last complete peal of 5040 changes I rang was on Sunday, the 9th June, 1907, at Billingshurst, performed in 2 hours 57 minutes, as follows:—

Percy Doick	...	...	treble
Albert Feist	...	...	2
Henry Burstow	...	...	3
William Stanford	...	...	4
Alfred Greenfield	...	...	5
William Short	...	...	6
George Woodman	...	...	7
John Rice	...	...	tenor

The bobs were called by William Short.

The following is a list of Belfries in which I have rung changes. Those marked with an asterisk are places where I have taught ringing :—

Horsham*	East Grinstead*
Angmering	Epsom
Arundel	Guildford
Balcombe*	Heene
Billingshurst*	Henfield
Blakemore	Horley*
Bolney	Hurstpierpoint
Bramber	Itchingfield*
Brighton—St. Peter's	Kirdford
„ St. Nicholas'†	Lewes—Southover
Broadwater	Lower Beeding*
Buxted	Lyminster
Capel*	Midhurst
Charlwood	Newdigate
Chiddingfold	Ockley
Cowfold	Petersfield
Cranleigh	Petworth
Crawley*	Ringmer
Cuckfield	Rudgwick
Dunsfold	Rusper*
Eastbourne—St. Saviour's	Ryde
„ Christ Church	Shalford

† When St. Nicholas, in 1777, first had eight bells, the Horsham ringers, who then enjoyed the reputation of being the best in Sussex, went and rung the first peal of 5040 changes on them.

H

Shere	Warnham*
Shipley*	Warpleston
Slinfold*	West Grinstead*
Steyning*	West Tarring
Storrington	Worth
Tunbridge Wells	

To all brother campanologists and friends who remain of the hundreds with whom I have had the pleasure of meeting and ringing in the above-mentioned belfries I hereby offer my kind regards, and thanks for the hearty welcome and good fellow-ship they have always shown me. Their friendship has helped to make light and easy my advance through every phase of life, and given me a very pleasant outlook upon human nature. I can, alas, never meet them in their belfries again, but should any of them ever come to Horsham I can give them a humble but warm welcome in my little room at 28, Spencer's Road, where we can still enjoy, at least, the recollections of some of the merry old peals we have pulled together, and where they can have a few songs from a heart still warm and firm if by a voice weakened by the inexorable operation of time. Peace to departed ringers whose bodies lie deaf to the de-lightful continuous sounds they once had a hand in creating; good luck to all who remain. That these latter may be blessed with good health, firm friend-ships, and cheerful circumstances as I have been, and maintain their interest in campanology, their delight in the merry bell and supple rope as I have always been able to do, shall be my sincere wish as long as I live.

SONGS AND SONG SINGING.

I do not know whether bell ringing or song singing has yielded me the greater pleasure through life. Whilst the former has been my sole physical exercise, except the compulsory ones of walking and stitching, the latter has been my chief mental delight, a delight that has been my companion day after day in my journey from infancy through every stage of life to my now extreme old age.

Song singing, too, was a great delight of my father's. He used to sing a great many songs, nearly two hundred. Of these he taught me all those starred in the following list, and from the hereditary start he gave me, from the time when but a mere child, I learnt at his knee my first song, "Travel the Country round," I have never ceased to obtain, and I hope seldom failed to give, satisfaction in this, the best mode I know of expressing the feelings.

In learning and retaining all my songs my memory has seemed to work quite spontaneously, in much the same way as the faculties of seeing and hearing: many of the songs I learnt at first time of hearing, others, longer ones, I have learnt upon hearing them twice through; none, not even "Tom Cladpole's trip to London," nor "Jan Cladpole's trip to 'Merricur," each of which has 155 verses, has ever given me any trouble to acquire. Besides those I learnt from my father, I also learnt several from my mother, and a great many more from various other people, my brother-in-law, Joe Hopkins, one of the old Horsham stone diggers, Harry Vaughan, bootmaker, who lived in the Causeway; Gaff Batchelor, tailor, Bishopric; Bob Boxall, labourer, Bishopric; Bill Strudwick, sailor, Bishopric; Jim Shoubridge, ex-soldier, Bishopric; Hoggy Mitchell, labourer, Bishopric; Richard Collins, the parish clerk, The Causeway; Michael Turner, bootmaker, Warnham; Tim Shoubridge, labourer, Bishopric; Jim Manvell, bricklayer, Queen Street. Jim could compose songs on any subject. "Now Jim, sing us a song about so and so," some one would ask, and perhaps in 20 minutes, or half an hour, Jim would have his new song ready, to which all were eager listeners. Besides these, many of the shoemakers, bellringers, and other workers with whom I came into contact, each and all of them knew several songs, and those to which I took a fancy I committed to memory: others again I learnt of "Country Wills" in the taprooms and parlours of public houses in the Town and Villages round, where song singing was always regularly indulged in during the evenings all the year round, and where the words of many songs have been taught and learnt, exchanged or sold, for perhaps a pint of beer. The remainder I learnt from ballad sheets I bought as they were being hawked about at the fairs, and at other times from other printed matter. I remember, when quite a boy, buying for my mother of a pedlar, as he sang in the street, the old ballad "Just before the battle, Mother." This was her favourite song because, I think, her brother, their mother's favourite boy, after having fought in many battles, had deserted and fled and was never more heard of. I have sung this song to her many times, never without bringing tears to her eyes; her last request to me as she lay on her death bed (she died 14th March, 1857) was to sing it to her again. It was this occasion—the occasion that can come but once in a lifetime—in which my prospective loss was measured by the depth of a mother's requited love, that I proved most fully the resources of my natural hobby as an outlet for expressions of the tenderest sentiments. I feel as sure as that I am myself awaited by death, that as she lay there, her hand in mine, with this her favourite song in her ear, nothing I could say or do, nor that anyone else could say or do could have better pleased or satisfied her last moments.

On all sorts of other occasions I have sung other songs, and there is not a village Inn for miles around Horsham where I have not sung one or more at a time. Wherever I went and sang I invariably got asked to come again; my songs never got stale to me nor, I believe, to my listeners, and I never got tired of singing them. On my 63rd birthday I walked to Rusper, counting the steps all the way, 10,611 in all, helped ring a peal of 5088 changes of treble bob major, sang twelve songs at the "Star Inn," and afterwards walked home. Some few times I have sung the list of 420 songs right through, every song from beginning to end; the last time I did so I sang them to my wife, commencing on the 4th April, 1906, the 78th anniversary of her birthday. I sang about ten on 41 consecutive evenings, and as we sat, evening after evening, one on either side of the fire, as happy as a king and queen, I singing my best, she listening and occasionally herself singing one of the fifty songs I had taught her, the old songs seemed as fresh and as pretty as they did when I first sang them fifty, sixty, perhaps seventy years or more ago. The most important public occasion I ever sang at was the Recreation Silver Band Concert on Thursday, the 12th March, 1908, at the King's Head Assembly Room, and I felt and still feel proud of the most intent and appreciative reception given me by that densely crowded room of people, the largest audience I ever sang to.

In 1892-3 I lent my list of songs to Miss Lucy E. Broadwood (later Hon. Secretary and Editor to the Folk Song Society), and sang to her a large number of them, which she noted. Miss Broadwood left her old home, "Lyne," near Horsham, in 1893, and some eleven years later suggested to Dr. Vaughan Williams, a country neighbour, that he should come to see me. I sang to him such songs as he asked for, all of which he took down; some of them he recorded by his phonograph. This was the first time I had seen or heard one of these marvellous machines, and I was amazed beyond expression to hear my own songs thus repeated in my own voice. Many of these songs have been printed in the Journal of the Folk Song Society, Part 4 of Vol. I., containing the largest number under one cover.

I am glad to know that in these ways have been preserved the words and tunes of nearly all those songs of mine that come within the objects of the Society, viz.: those that are " traditional survivals " of songs expressive of the thoughts and emotions of " untaught people passing between mind and mind " from more or less remote periods to the present " time."*

Some of them have been published, with the tunes harmonized, by Miss Broadwood, and can now be bought in cheap book form, viz.: " English County Songs " (published by the Leadenhall Press Ltd.), and " English Traditional Songs and Carols " (published by Boosey & Co.). A shilling edition of the latter brings many of my songs within reach of all, and contains a large proportion of Sussex and Surrey songs noted elsewhere by Miss Broadwood.

Since the publication of my songs in the above-mentioned books other collectors have called and

---

* This definition of Folk Song (source unknown) meets with the approval of the Hon. Secretary of the Folk Song Society.

noted songs from me with a view to the publication of them.

I give a list of my songs at end. I can sing any and all of them now, and still entertain myself nearly every day, and friends occasionally, by singing some of them. The other day I sang over forty; another time I amused myself with "Tom Cladpole's Trip to London" and "Jan Cladpole's Trip to Merricur," and so I continue daily to exact a pleasant tribute from my life-long hobby. This day, Thursday, the 12th October, 1911, I recited "A Parting Address to Horsham" to a young friend of mine, who is leaving the town for London. And as I now feel I, too, before many years must be leaving the town and take that longer journey that lies before all of us, I cannot do better than give my readers, as a sincere farewell, that very pretty piece of poetry, written about 1835 by a young girl, words that express much better than any of my own, my affection for my dear old native town of Horsham.

A PARTING ADDRESS TO HORSHAM.
By Miss M. E. DUDLEY.

Horsham, dear Town, in thee no more I dwell,
To thee, alas, I now must bid farewell.
A native spot hast thou appeared to me,
But now, for ever, I must part from thee;
And when far distant from thee, much-loved place,
Fond memory's tear shall oft bedew my face,
With fancied pleasure shall I call to mind
The long lost scenes that I have left behind.
The ancient Church, with monumental art,
Sculptured o'er those once dearest to the heart;
Whose spire, erecting high its taper form,
Has braved and still encounters many a storm;
Whose bells at evening, with sudden swell,
Oft pealed with merry change, or rung the knell
Of some departed spirit, flown away
To realms of endless night, or everlasting day.
The pleasant walk along the churchyard paths,
Where oft we've pondered on the epitaphs
Of those whose bones have crumbled into dust,
Removed from pain and every sinful lust.

And oft I'll think upon the small cascade,
Where foaming waters musically played;
And where the stately swan, with head elate,
Led out upon the river his fair mate.
Sometimes we walked beside the Water Mill,
Still oftener saunter'd up the sunny hill,
Plucking wild flowers, which around us grew—
Forget-me-not and modest violet blue.
On the hill-top a grassy mound we view,
And at its base a pond of greenish hue:
All spread beneath, displayed before the eyes,
The neat and pleasant town of Horsham lies.
There have I watched the gentle leveret leap
Amidst the glen so dark, so lone, so steep,
Springing above the purple heath and fern,
With fearful timorous glance at every turn.
Sometimes we pushed the clustering leaves aside
To gather of the green bank's rosy pride
The ruddy strawberry, wild, yet good to eat,
Rural repast, and therefore doubly sweet.
Oft have I listened to the sounds which there
Rose up the hill and mingled with the air:
The cattle lowing in the grassy mead,
Where, mid the golden buttercups, they feed;
The bleating sheep in distant flowery dells,
And soothing murmur of the rural bells,
The simple sighing of the summer breeze,
Which gently murmured through the lofty trees
That rear their mossy stems and branches high
And spread their greenest foliage to the sky;
Such sounds infused a quiet in the mind,
And left tumultuous, jarring thoughts behind.
Horsham! the attachment that I have for thee,
Shall never from my heart effaced be.
So, when two friends are forced by death to part,
To rend affections tie from each fond heart;
He who is left behind reflects with pain,
He ne'er on earth shall see his friend again,
Remembers all is ordered for the best,
And patiently resigns to God the rest.
How many who, when here we came to dwell,
Were strong and lively, vigorous and well,
Are now all mingled with that silent earth,
To whose parental soil they owed their birth.
Horsham! how often have I wished my bones
May crumble near thy Church, beneath its stones;
But now remote from thee I go to dwell,
To thee, alas, I now repeat, farewell.

Farewell! what says that sad word to the heart;
It, household, kindred friends hath torn apart.
The mariner, in sailing from the strand,
Breathes a sad farewell to his native land.
The dying man, to those who round him kneel,
Sighs with his parting breath farewell! farewell!!
The exile, sailing from his native shore,
Drops memory's tear to those he sees no more,
And sighs farewell! the while he calls to mind
The numerous relatives he's left behind.
So will I drop a tear to thee, loved town,
Where many years of happiness I've known;
But ever if within my power it lies,
A second sight of thee shall glad mine eyes.
I'll view once more a place to me so dear;
Retrace each favourite haunt, forgotten ne'er
The visit which in summer we had paid,
But which again by us shall ne'er be made—
To Stroud, where hospitality was found,
Where kindness, uniform, we met around.
In journeying, want of chariot was supplied
By cover'd cart, where splendour was denied;
Instead of steed, caparisoned and gay,
A steady cart horse drew us on our way.
And as the vehicle moved slowly on
We cheered ourselves with merry laugh or song;
And when at length we reached the rural place,
Unfeigned pleasure beamed in every face.
With joy they welcomed us to their retreat,
Where all was homely, but 'twas clean and neat.
I fancy now the dame, whose cottage old,
Her poverty but neatness plainly told;
Within her kitchen, with its red-bricked floor,
Our board was spread—that festive scene is o'er.
Near her abode an aged couple dwelt,
Who long the infirmities of age had felt;
Their daughter with them lived, on them bestowed
The attentive duty which to them she owed.
Along her garden sweet I loved to stray,
To inhale the fragrance of the summer's day.
Her father, now all nature's debt had paid,
His bones beneath the grassy sod are laid;
Few of his merits e'er to us were known,
But hospitality was always shewn.
The steady horse, whose back and shoulders broad,
Were often destined for a heavier load
(Without a saddle on his back we rode).
Traversed the shady lane and sunny field,
And gather'd wild flowers, half by grass concealed.

Nor can I here forget the noble park,
With its tall grove of trees, so thick and dark.
We also were permitted to explore
The garden, and partake its liberal store
Of fruit, and view the fine extensive grounds,
Indulged with sight of poultry and the hounds.
We visited the fishing house, which stands
Raised o'er the pond, whose bosom wide expands,
Rippling and circling in the golden ray
As if exulting in the glow of day.
That day by us with joy was ever spent,
To Stroud with cheerful glee we always went.
At length returning from this lovely place,
Our steps to th' humble cottage we retrace,
And shared the social meal of home-made bread,
With pleasant fresh-churned butter on it spread;
Refreshing tea with cream scarce one day old,
Meantime the dame some ancient legend told.
Quickly the time drew near when we must part,
And leave this rural dwelling for our cart.
And bidding farewell to the ancient dame,
Wishing her health, and she to us the same.
We left the cot, not thinking that we ne'er
Again should enter it, or that from dear
Regretted Horsham, we so soon must roam,
When we must leave for ever this our home.
But though remote from thee I go to dwell,
Though now to thee I'm forced to bid farewell,
Thy memory from my heart, by Lethe's stream,
Shall ne'er be chased, or vanish like a dream.
To view thy landscape, press thy flowery dell,—
These scenes are past, dear Horsham! fare thee well.

M. E. D.

LIST OF SONGS.

1 Boney's farewell to Paris.	*12 The Old Deserter.
*2 Boney in St. Helena.	13 The New Deserter
*3 Boney's Lamentation.	*14 Stinston the Deserter.
4 Deeds of Napoleon.	15 The Sailor's Dream.
5 Dream of Napoleon.	*16 Mary's Dream.
*6 The Grand Conversation of	17 The Wife's Dream.
Napoleon.	18 The Husband's Dream.
7 The Soldier's Dream.	19 I had a Dream.
8 The Soldier's Tear.	*20 The Battle of Waterloo.
9 The tired Soldier.	*21 The Battle of Barrosa.
10 The poor worn out Soldier.	*22 The Battle of America.
11 The Old Soldier's Daughter.	23 The Standard Bearer.

24 Up with the Standard of England.
25 Mother, is the Battle o'er?
26 The Answer to it.
*27 The Wounded Hussar.
*28 Allen's Return from the Wars.
29 The Rose of Allandale.
30 The Rose of Britain's Isle.
31 She wore a Wreath of Roses.
32 Ben Bolt.
33 Ben Bolt's Reply.
34 Tom Bowling.
*35 Tom Hillyard.
*36 Tom Tough.
*37 Will Watch.
38 Harry Hawser.
*39 Paul Jones.
40 John William Marchant
41 Gibson, Wilson, and Johnson.
42 Gilderoy.
*43 Auld Robin Gray.
44 Answer to ditto.
45 Barney Avouring.
46 Joe the Marine.
47 John Lawrence.
48 Ditto second part.
*49 Larry O' Gaff.
50 Beautiful Kitty.
51 Kathleen Mavourneen.
52 Sarah had a little Lamb.
53 Helen Lorraine.
54 My Helen is the Fairest Flower.
55 Dear Charlotte when the Sun is Set.
*56 Alice Gray.
57 Fanny Gray.
58 Nelly Gray.
59 Mrs. Myrtle.
60 Grace Darling.
61 Birth of Crazy Jane.
62 Crazy Jane.
63 Death of Crazy Jane.
64 Jeannette and Jeannot.
65 The Answer.
66 Pretty Phoebe.
67 Pretty Susan, the Pride of Kildare.

68 Annie Laurie.
69 Bristol Town.
70 Gentle Annie.
*71 I am leaving Thee in sorrow, Annie.
72 Lost Rosabel,
73 Minnie.
74 Little Nell.
75 Mary of Argyle.
76 Mary Blane.
*77 Mary was a Beauty.
*78 Sally, Sally one Day.
79 Poor Uncle Tom.
80 Uncle Ned.
81 Green Mossy Banks of the Lee.
*82 Ye Banks and Braes of Bonny Doon.
83 Ye Banks of Bonny Winding Tyne.
*84 Banks of the Dee.
85 Woodman Spare that Tree.
86 Butcher Spare that Lamb.
87 My good Old Father's Mill.
88 My good Old Father's Farm.
89 The Old House at Home.
90 Home, Sweet Home.
91 The Rover.
*92 Banks of Sweet Dundee.
93 The Star of Glengarry.
94 The Maid of Llangollen.
95 We have Lived and Loved Together.
96 My Skiff is by the Shore.
*97 Adieu, my Native Land, Adieu.
*98 Old England, what are you Coming to?
99 Britain's Revenge on the Death of Nelson.
100 Madam, do you know my Trade is War.
101 How Sweet in the Woodland.
102 Oh no, I never mention Her.
103 The Answer to It.
*104 In Essex there lived a rich Farmer.

105 Oh cease, awhile, ye Winds to Blow.
106 The Answer to it.
*107 When I was Young and in my Prime.
108 Yarmouth is a Pretty Town.
109 Its of a Sailor now I write.
110 The Lass of Brighton Town
111 Polly's Love, or the Cruel Ship's Carpenter.
112 Rosetta and the Plough Boy.
*113 The Old Man and his three Daughters.
*114 Flora, the Unkind Shepherdess.
115 Our Captain calls all Hands.
116 Isle of Beauty, fare Thee well.
117 Wealthy Farmer's Son.
118 The Constant Farmer's Son.
119 I will be a Gipsy.
120 The Gipsy's Tent.
121 Fitzgerald's Tent.
122 Jervis' Tent.
123 The Irish Emigrant.
124 The Answer to it.
*125 Lango Lee.
*126 Exile of Erin.
127 Leather Breeches.
128 Miser Grimes.
129 One Night I went to meet Her.
130 Old Gray Mare.
*131 Mark and John Peteroe.
132 Old Dog Tray.
133 Poor Black Bess.
134 Bonny Black Bess.
*135 Bonny Moon.
*136 The Storm.
137 The Minute Gun at Sea.
138 The Female Smuggler.
139 Highland Mary.
140 My Highland Home.
*141 'Ere around the Huge Oak.
142 The Oak Table.

143 A Song to the Oak.
144 The Effects of Love.
*145 The Green Hills of Tyrol.
146 Cabbage Green.
*147 Belfast Mountains.
148 A Week's Matrimony.
149 Umbrella Courtship.
*150 The Croppy Boy.
151 The Sailor's Return.
152 The Lovers Parting.
153 New York Street.
*154 Plato's Advice.
155 Dulce Domum.
*156 Through Moorfields.
*157 On Gosport Beach.
*158 The Gallant Poachers.
159 The Gallant Sailor.
160 Creeping Jane.
161 Death and the Lady.
162 The Scarlet Flower.
*163 The Post Captain.
*164 The Cabin Boy.
165 Gooseberry Wine.
*166 Travel the Country Round.
*167 The Age of Man.
168 The Sailor Boy's Good-bye.
196 Angel's Whisper.
*170 Spare a Halfpenny.
171 Some love to Roam.
172 The Blackbird.
173 The Woodpecker.
174 Our Bessie was a Sailor's Bride.
175 As I was a Walking one Morning by Chance.
176 The Salt Sea.
177 The Pitcher.
178 The Haymakers.
179 The Marble Halls.
*180 The Sheffield Apprentice.
*181 The London Apprentice.
182 The Fairy Tempter.
183 After Roving Many Years.
184 All's Well.
185 Annie Lisle.
186 The Plough Boy.
187 Night and-Morn.
188 O Lovely Night.
189 The little Town Boy.

*190 Robin Hood and the Pedlar.
*191 Past Ten O'clock.
*192 The Cobbler.
193 The Kiss dear Maid.
194 The Irish Girl's Lament.
195 The Boyhood Days.
*196 The Galley Slave.
197 Rosemary Lane.
198 In a Cottage near a Wood.
199 You Combers All.
200 The Young Jockey.
201 Little Cupid.
202 The Last Rose of Summer.
203 Four and Nine.
204 The Tarry Sailor.
205 The Bridal Ring.
*206 Banstead Downs.
*207 The Pilot.
208 The Mariner's Grave.
209 I have Journeyed over many Lands.
*210 Our Trade and Commerce.
211 The Miller's Three Sons.
212 The Cavalier.
213 Salisbury Plain.
214 To all you Ladies now on Land.
215 Nature's Gay Days.
216 The Demon of the Seas.
217 He is gone to the Roaring Waves.
*218 The Wild Rover.
219 Vilikins and Dinah.
220 The Troubadour.
221 Shells of the Ocean.
222 Oh, come to the Ingleside.
223 Give me but a Cot in the Valley I love.
224 Cherry Cheek Polly for Me.
*225 When the Morn stands on Tiptoe.
226 The Cot where I was Born.
227 The Orphan Beggar Boy.
228 Red, White, and Blue.
*229 The Cottager's Daughter.
230 Old Folks at Home.
231 The Convict's Lamentation.
232 Butter, Cheese, and All.

233 With all thy Faults I love Thee still.
234 Wait for the Waggon.
235 Oh Willie, we have missed you.
236 Rouse! Brother, Rouse.
*237 Partant Pour la Syrie.
238 I'll hang my Harp on a Willow Tree.
239 The Heart and Hand.
240 The Basket of Eggs.
241 Will you love Me then as now?
242 Dearest, then, I'll love Thee now.
243 Old Towler.
244 When Other Lips.
245 Pretty Wench.
246 No Mistake in that.
247 The Beggar Girl.
248 My Gentle Mother Dear.
249 Isle of France.
250 The Little Bird.
*251 The American Stranger.
252 Quite Politely.
253 Tally Ho.
254 The Light of Other Days.
255 The Bay of Biscay.
256 The Lass O'Gowry.
257 Good News from Home.
258 Beautiful Star.
259 The Queen's Letter.
260 Nothing More.
261 Tempest of the Heart.
262 The Rent Days.
263 Abroad as I was Walking.
264 Down in those Meadows.
265 A Voice from the West.
266 To the West.
267 Ploughman turned Sailor.
*268 Old Carrion Crow.
269 The Sailor's Tear.
270 Why did She Leave Him.
271 Prairie Child.
272 Good-Bye Sweetheart
*273 Peggy Ban.
*274 Duke of Marlborough.
275 The Young Recruit.
276 The Mistletoe Bough.

277 The Song of the Brave.
278 All among the Barley.
279 The Sons of Fingal.
*280 The Blue Bells of Scotland.
281 The Happy Land.
282 The Poor Fisherman's Boy.
283 So Early in the Morning.
284 Hard Times come again no more.
285 Farewell to the Mountains.
286 Thou art gone from my Gaze.
287 The Banks of the Blue Moselle.
*288 The Months of the Year.
289 The Blighted Flower.
290 The Officer's Funeral.
291 The Sailor's Grave.
292 Cheer, Boys, Cheer.
293 Ever of Thee.
294 Kitty Terrell.
295 Popping the Question.
296 Aunt Sally.
297 Jemima Brown.
298 Maid of Judah.
299 The Gipsy Girl.
*300 Not a Drum was Heard.
*301 My old Friend John.
*302 Benbow.
303 Down in the Cornfields.
304 Meet Me by Moonlight Alone.
305 The Cottage by the Sea.
306 Your Lot is far above Me.
*307 A Rose Tree in full Bearing.
308 The Merry Mountain Horn.
309 Fair Lily of the Vale.
310 Kathleen O'Moore.
311 Where there's a Will there's a Way.
312 Oh Bitter and Cold was the Night.
313 Sweet Spirit, Hear my Prayer.
314 Oh would I were a Bird.
315 The Hazel Dell.
316 Happy as a King.
317 Father, dear Father, come Home with Me now.

318 Beautiful Isle of the Sea.
319 Maid of Erin's Isle.
320 The Gleaner.
321 The Bride's Farewell.
*322 Harry Bluff.
323 The Sicilian Maid.
324 The Village Born Beauty.
*325 Jenny Jones.
326 Fifty Years Ago.
327 Nothing shall she Draw, but Water from the Well.
328 The Glasses Sparkled on the Board.
329 Norah, Sweet Norah.
330 My Friend and Pitcher.
331 The Minstrel Boy.
332 The Thorn.
333 You Lads and Lasses Gay.
334 The Ivy Cottage.
335 Water Cresses.
336 Jimmy and Jenny.
337 Banks of Sweet Primroses.
338 Canadian Boat Song.
339 False One, I love Thee still.
340 William and Phyllis.
341 The Grecian Bend.
*342 Billy and Sally.
343 After tasting many Beers.
344 I'll meet Thee at the Lane.
345 Wait for the Turn of the Tide.
*346 The Heart that can feel for Another.
347 The Captain and His Whiskers.
348 Just before the Battle, Mother.
349 Just after the Battle, Mother.
350 I am come across the Seas.
351 The Female Sailor.
*352 Goddess Diana.
353 Green Bushes.
354 Bold Collins
355 O Leave not your Kathleen.
356 Sir Roger Tichborne.
357 Come Back to Erin.

358 The Gipsy's Warning.
359 The Answer to ditto.
360 The Maiden's Reply.
361 The Merry Bells of England.
362 Far Far Away.
363 Broker, spare that Bed.
364 Kitty Wells.
365 Sunshine follows Rain.
366 Write Me a Letter from Home.
367 Dublin Bay.
368 Belle Mahone.
369 Molly Darling.
370 Annie dear, I am called away.
*371 In the Downhill of Life.
372 When first in this Country a Stranger I came.
373 As I was going to Birmingham Fair.
374 Nancy Lee.
375 Silver Threads Among the Gold.
376 The Rat-catcher's Daughter.
377 Ring the Bell, Watchman.
378 Barrel of Beer.
379 Go and leave Me if You wish.
380 Put Me in my little Bed.
*381 Auld Lang Syne.
*382 As I wandered by the Brookside.
*383 Make little Mary his Bride.
384 It was just against the Gate.
385 Away with Melancholy.
386 *Black Eyed Susan.
387 Good Old Jeff.
388 The Negro Boy.
*389 With my Pot in one Hand.
390 Nature's Holiday.
391 Won't you buy my pretty Flowers.

392 That dear old Stile.
393 The Crocodile.
*394 The American has Stole my true Love away.
395 Begone Dull Care.
396 The Harp that once through Tara's Hall.
397 An Old Man came Courting Me.
*398 The Holy Friar.
399 Bread and Cheese and Kisses.
400 There came to Enslave us a Landlord of Erin.
401 The Garden Gate.
402 Joan and the Miller.
403 The Primrose Lass.
404 Roger and Flora.
405 The Devil He Came to an Old Man at the Plough.
406 The Brighton Chain Pier.
407 The Second Part ditto.
408 Bonny Bunch of Roses.
409 The North Fleet weighed Anchor.
410 The 18th June.
411 Duke William.
412 We wassailing Lads are Come.
413 As I was walking one morning in May.
414 Jerry Brown and the Black Jug.
415 The Tavern.
416 The Donkey.
417 John Cladpole's Trip to London.
418 Tom Cladpole's Trip to America.
419 St. Nicholas Church.
420 Turnips are Round.

LIST OF SUBSCRIBERS.

Agate, A. T., Horsham
Agate, Stephen, Horsham
Albery, Miss Rose, Boston, U.S.A.
Albery, Miss Ruth, Horsham
Aldridge, Norman, Horsham
Aldridge, R. H., Horsham
Aliss, Wm. J., Henfield
Anderson, Miss M., Brighton
Anderson, W. H., Horsham
Apedaile, Ernest G., Horsham
Arnold, Miss L., Horsham
Arundel, J. W., Horsham
Attree, Chas. Jno., Horsham
   (6 copies)
Attwater, Arthur L., Horsham
Attwater, H. C., Horsham

Bachelor, W., Capel
Bailey, Alf., Two-Mile-Ash
Bailey, Wm., Horsham
Baker, Arthur, Horsham
Baker, Arthur J., Kenora, Canada
Baker, Bernard T., Horsham
Balchin, W., Horsham
Bampton, H., Horsham
Barrett, Sylvester, Christ's Hospital
Baverstock, E. A., Horsham
Berry, Oscar, C.C., F.C.A., Seaview,
   Isle of Wight
Bishop, The Misses A. and C.,
   Bournemouth
Blaber, Wm. H., Hove (2 copies)
Blackman, Benj., Horsham
Blackmore, W., Horsham
Blunt, Wilfrid Scawen, Shipley
   (5 copies)
Bolwell, J., Horsham
Bond, Rev. John, M.A., Horsham
Botting, Mrs. Robt., Brockenhurst
Bourn, Mrs. Rd., Horsham
Boyd, W. H., Horsham
Brackebusch, Mrs., Horsham
   (2 copies)
Brandt, Alfred, Bournemouth

Brassington, H. W., Horsham
Broad, J. S., Horsham
   (2 copies)
Broadwood, Miss Lucy, London
   (2 copies)
Brooke, Miss, Horsham
Browne, C. E., Horsham
Bryant, C. A., Horsham
Bryce, David, Horsham
Budd, B., Shipley (2 copies)
Bull, Joseph Cecil, Stevenage
Burchell, W., Slinfold
Burdfield, J., Billingshurst
Burstow, Chas. H., Horsham
Burt, A., Horsham
Butler, F. S. W., Gainsborough
Buttemer, R. W., Godalming
Buttifant, J. G., Horsham

Capon, H. F., Horsham
Charman, Alf., British Columbia
Charman, C., Southend
Charman, Miss E., Horsham
Charman, Tom, New Forest
Chart, L. J., Horsham
Churchman, Miss, Horsham
Clarke, F., Horsham
Clifford, H. W., Horsham
Combridge, S., Hove
Cook, E., Horsham
Coole, Arthur C., Horsham
Corbett, W. H., Horsham
Cotching, T., Horsham
Cramp, Arthur, Horsham
Cramp, Jury, Horsham
Cramp, Walter, Horsham
Cripps, A., Shipley
Cripps, F. W., Kingsfold
Crowhurst, R. W., Horsham

Davis, Mrs. M. J., High Barnet
Dean, John, Horsham
Dench, W. E., Horsham
Dendy, A. W., Horsham
Dendy, Geo. F., Horsham

I

Dendy, Mrs. Geo., Horsham
Dewdney, G. W., Horsham
Dewdney, R., Slinfold
Dewing, Maurice, Horsham
Dinnage, H., Horsham
Doick, P., Pulborough
Doick, H., Pulborough
Duffield, Mrs. H., Ontario

Eager, Percy Geo., Horsham
Edwards, E., Slinfold
Elliott, T. H., Horsham
Ellis. Miss M. F., Horsham
Elms, Miss F. H., Horsham
Elton, Miss Ida, Hammersmith

Fawn, Miss, Horsham
Fawn, W. H., Horsham
Fox, Mrs., Horsham
Freeman, J., Horsham

Garner, Joseph, Horsham
Gates, W., Horsham
Gill, W. H., Angmering
Glaysher, T., Horsham
Glaysher, Wm. G., Nuthurst
Goldsmith, J. S., Woking
Green, A. W., Hailsham
Greenfield, Edward, Horsham
Greenfield, Geo. O., Fulham
Greenin, Miss, Horsham
Groves, J. E., Birmingham
Gurney, Miss V. I., Towcester

Halloway, Miss, Horsham
Halls, Mrs. W. E., New Forest
Hancock, C. O., Horsham
Hawes, E. C., Horsham
Hecks, Mrs. E. B., Horsham
Hemsley, Miss F., Horsham
Henwood, Roger, Horsham
Hewell, J. W., Horsham
Hird, Rev. Francis Fraser, M.A.,
    Bournemouth
Hoad, A. E., Birmingham
Hoad, F. W., Weybridge
Hoad, W. J., Horsham (2 copies)
Hobden, Mrs., Horsham
Holloway, A., Slinfold
Hooker, Mrs. H. M., Horsham
Hopgood, Frank, Horsham

Horsham Bellringers (per Leo.
    Paice)
Hudson, Robert Louth, Horsham
Hull, Miss H., Horsham
Hunt, Albert A., Horsham
Hunt, Arthur, Horsham
Hunt, H. Cyril, Horsham
Hunt, Jas., Guildford

Ings, Mrs. H., Brighton
Ireland, Frank, Horsham

Johnston, A. A., Croydon
Jones, G. Selkirk, L.S.A., Horsham
Jupp, George, Slinfold
Jupp, S. H., Nabawa, W. Australia

Kay, Claude, Horsham
Kempson, Arthur J. T., Horsham
Kensett, Miss Emily, Horsham
Kensett, Miss Elizth. J., Horsham
Kensett, Walter Wm., Horsham
Kent, Fred, Horsham
Kent, Thos., Horsham
Kerr, W. J., Horsham
Killick, J. Morton, Hendon
Killner, A., Slinfold
King, Mrs. Geo., Guildford
King, Miss, Guildford
King, J. Reg., Horsham
King, L., Bexhill-on-Sea
King, W., Horsham
King, W. W., Horsham
Kinneir, Mrs. F. W. E., Horsham
Kittle, E. J., Horsham
Knight, A., Horsham
Knight, A., Rusper
Knight, Elias, Slinfold
Knight, Percy Wm., Horsham
Knott, Horace T., Horsham

Laker, Miss, Horsham
Lampard, J. T. H., Horsham
Lane, E. T., Horsham
Lane, Wm., Roffey
Laughton, C. S., Horsham
Lawrence, E. E., Horsham
Lawrence, H., Horsham
Leppard, W., Horsham
Lewry, F., Nuthurst
Lindfield, Wm., Horsham

Lintott, Wm. Hy. Bernard, Horsham
Lower, A. F., Horsham
Lucas, C. J., Warnham Court

Maides, E. A., Horsham
Markwell, Wm., Henfield
Marten, Rev. J. J., Horsham
Martin, Miss H., Horsham
Martin, Percy T., Horsham
Martin, T. W., Horsham
Masters, Rev. Geo. E. F., M.A., Bournemouth
Michell, Guy, West Worthing
Michell, Herbert, Stamford Hill
Mills, Henry, Horsham
Mills, Miss L., Horsham
Mitchell, G. S., Horsham (2 copies)
Mitchell, Samuel, Horsham (2 copies)
Mitchell, Walter E., Horsham
Mockford, Geo., Horsham
Moody, M., Horsham
Moor, Rev. Fredk., B.D., Horsham
Moore, John H., Liverpool
Morgan, Edwd. Miall, Port Talbot, South Wales
Morgan, J. B., Horsham

Nailard, Mrs. J., Horsham
Nelson, Miss K., Crawley
Netley, J., Arundel
Neville, E., Horsham
Nye, W., Horsham

Oakley, Geo., Horsham
Oldershaw, Ernest, Horsham
Osborne, N. C., York
Ottaway, Ernest W., London.
Owers, W., Horsham

Page, Chas., Horsham
Paice, G., Lower Edmonton
Parker, F., Horsham
Parsons, G. H., Horsham
Pearce, Ernest W., Horsham
Peirce, W., West Grinstead
Penfold, Miss E., Chertsey
Penfold, George, Pevensey
Phillips, C. A., Horsham
Philpot, John, Horsham

Pierce, Mrs. Robt., Cambridge
Pierce, A., Horsham
Piffard, E. J. G., Horsham
Piffard, Miss Mary, Brockenhurst
Pigott, H. J., Horsham
Potter, Miss, Horsham
Potter, Geo., Horsham
Potter, Jas., Horsham
Pratt, Miss H. E., Horsham
Pratt, H. J., Horsham
Pratt, Miss L. A., Ontario
Pratt, Miss M., Ontario
Pratt, Wm. C., Oxford
Prewett, Bertram, Watford
Prewett, Wm., Horsham
Price, D. M. G., F.E.S., Horsham (2 copies)
Price, James Brent, Horsham
Pullen, Alfred, Horsham
Pullen, J., Rudgwick
Puttock, A. H., Horsham
Puttock, G. J., Horsham

Rapley, W. G., Slinfold
Rawlison, Alfred W., Horsham
Reynolds, F. L., Horsham
Rice, R. Garraway, J.P., F.S.A., Pulborough
Richardson, A. Ernest, Ramsgate
Richardson, Chas. V., Saffron Walden
Robinson, Miss Emilie, Boxmoor
Rowland, Chas., Horsham
Rowland, Gerald, Horsham
Rowland, Mrs. Gerald, Horsham
Rowland, S. E., Horsham

Sapey, F. D., Horsham
Savage, Miss, Horsham
Sayer, Miss, Horsham
Sayers, J. H., Horsham (2 copies)
Scott, A. H., Horsham
Scutt, F. J., Horsham
Seagrave, Mrs. Elizth., Horsham
Seagrave, Fredk., Horsham
Seymour, G. F., Horsham
Sendall, Frank A., Horsham
Sendall, Fredk. Evershed, Horsham
Sendall, Geo. H., Horsham
Sendall, Wm. F., Horsham

Sheppard, Miss A., Horsham
Shoubridge, F. C., Horsham
Simmonds, Miss C. A., Southwick
Simmonds, W., Horsham
Skinner, Mrs. Elizabeth, Horsham
Sleeman, F., Horsham
Snelling, D. W., Epsom
Smallwood, Mrs. H., King's Langley
Smith, F. Turner, Southwater
Smith, Herbert, Roffey
Society of Genealogists of London (per Chas. A. Bernau)
Spratt, Rd. Henry Hamilton, Bournemouth
Squire, Miss G. M., Horsham
Stanford, Geo. F., Horsham
Stanford, Oliver Alfred, Horsham
Stanford, W., Slinfold
Stedman, Alfred Jas., Horsham
Stedman, Arthur, A R.I.B.A., Chattanooga, Tennessee, U.S.A.
Stedman, Fredk., M.R.C.S., Leighton Buzzard
Stedman, Herman, F.R.C.S., Hendon
Stedman, Jas., L.R.C.P., Bournemouth
Stedman, Jas. Athelstane, Epsom College
Stedman, P. T. H., M.B., Leighton Buzzard
Stedman, T. Gurney, Horsham
Stedman, Thos. Bernard, M.D., Selby
Stephens, J. H., Horsham
Stott, Chas. Jno., Horsham
Strettell, W. J., Broadbridge Heath
Summerfield, Joseph, Horsham

Tanner, H., Horsham
Tate, James, Horsham

Taylor, Edward, Horsham
Taylor, E. J. W., Horsham
Thompson. A. G. G., Horsham
Thompson, Rev. Geo. Alfred, M.A., LL.D., Horsham
Theobald, J., Horsham
Thorpe, Miss, Horsham
Thorpe, Miss K., Horsham
Thorpe, Miss N., Horsham
Tobitt, J., Horsham
Tolmie, Miss F., Edinburgh
Townsend, Lewis W., Horsham
Trimble, Mrs. J. A., Horsham
Trotter, Geo., Storrington
Tyler, Chas., Henfield

Vaughan, Chas., Horsham
Vincent, Wm. J., Bolney

Walder, Geo., jun., Bolney
Walker, J. W., Horsham
Wallis, H., Horsham
Welti, Mrs. Adolf, Berne, Switzerland
Waugh, Rev. Adam, Horsham
Weller, E., Horsham
Weller. Frank, Horsham
Wheeldon, J. E., Stoke-on-Trent
Whitburn, Mrs.. Guildford
Whiting, F. J., Horsham
Whittington, Mrs. R., Cranleigh
Willett, J., Horsham
Windwood, Thos., Horsham
Winterton, Earl, M.P., London
Woodman, Mrs. A., Boscombe
Woollan, J. H., Horsham
Worley, Miss E., Ealing

Young, Rev. A. F., Rudgwick

CONTENTS.

INDEX OF NAMES.